Luciana Savelli

SICILY
History and Masterpieces

500 COLOR PHOTOS · MAP OF SICILY

BONECHI EDIZIONI "IL TURISMO"

Distributor for Sicily:
PROMOLIBRI
di Luigi Zangara & C. S.a.s.
Via Aquileia, 84
90144 Palermo
Tel. +39-091.6702413 - Fax +39-091.6703633

© Copyright 2005 by Bonechi - Edizioni "Il Turismo" S.r.l.
Via G. Di Vittorio, 31 - 50145 Firenze
Tel. +39-055.375739/3424527
Fax +39-055.374701
E-mail: bbonechi@dada.it
        info@bonechionline.com
http://www.bonechionline.com

Publishing manager: Barbara Bonechi
The texts "That prodigious Baroque" and "Antonello, comet of Messina" are by: Alessandro Listri
Editorial coordination, revision of texts, iconographic research: Lorena Lazzari
Cover, design and graphics: Paola Rufino
Photographic references: **Melo Minnella** (Palermo);
Fotostudio Piero Orlandi (Lainate - Milan): pages 4 (above left), 27 (below), 85 (above), 103 (below right), 113 (center and right), 124 (above center and right), 146 (above), 148 (below right), 162 (above and center), 166 (below), 173 (below), 174 (above), 182 (center);
Massimo Listri (Florence): pages 20, 22 (above), 23, 30 (below right), 31 (above), 33, 46, 47 (above and center), 144 (below left);
Carfagna & Associati (Rome): pages 5 (below right), 36 (above), 44 (below left), 76 (above), 100 (below), 153 (above right);
Regista teatrale Beppe Ghiglioni (Florence): pages 63 (above left and center), 160 (below), 161 (below right), 179 (below right);
Publisher's Archives (Bonechi Edizioni "Il Turismo" S.r.l.).
The plan of Sicily was kindly granted by: Edizioni Multigraphic S.r.l. - Florence - www.edizionimultigraphic.it
English translation: Erika Pauli, Studio Comunicare
Photolithography: Puntoeacapo, Florence
Printing: Lito Terrazzi, Florence

The Publishing House and the Author thank the Region of Sicily, all the Tourist Boards and Pro Loco of the territory for their collaboration and helpfulness.

The Author particularly thanks her children: Alessandro, Benedetta, Maria Sole and Allegra for their help.

ISBN: 88-7204-579-7

* The location of the artworks in this book corresponds to their whereabouts as the book goes to press.
* Everything possible has been done to ascertain the legitimate owners of the rights for individual illustrations.
 In case there have been involuntary omissions, we will be happy to pay the user fees.

AMAZING SICILY

esare Brandi begins his book, "Sicilia mia" by asking whether a trip to Sicily could ever be seen as anything but a reward or the fulfilment of a vow. For indeed a visit to this extraordinary land is an unforgettable and highly gratifying experience. Sicily is seductive and turbulent, exciting and alluring but it also keeps the visitor at a distance. Sicily is the land of a thousand faces, a thousand souls, a thousand panoramas, history and myth, agony and rebirth, splendor and desolation. In its contrasts and contradictions truth seems to lie in what is apparent, but the contradictions, here the rule, express the multiple aspects of its nature and sum up all the charm and uniqueness of this island.

Sicily is green, fertile, flourishing, the garden of the Mediterranean, with citrus groves, carobs, pistachios, palm trees, and exotic plants bursting into bloom.

Sicily is harsh and barren, its hinterland cracked open by the African sun, yellow with a sulphurous dust. But it is also a land of softly rolling hills with fields of wheat. Sicily is a transparent sea, blue and African, with a jagged coastline, tropical white and black lava beaches. Sicily is snow-capped white mountains and the black volcanoes of Stromboli, Vulcano and Etna, the largest and most spectacular of European volcanoes. What strikes one most though is the light, a white light, enveloping but sometimes violent, and the scirocco, the southeast wind from Africa, unnerving and clammy, that on certain days turns the sky indaco, and the climate where spring comes in February and summer ends in December.

▼ The endless vistas of the Sicilian countryside, sea and mountains.

▼ Mongerbino from Solunto, a unique Sicilian landscape.

▲ Mount Etna, Sicily's volcano.

▲ The Temple of Concord
in the Valley of the Temples.

▲ The famous Greek Theater in Taormina.

There is a Western Sicily, regal and voluptuous, sumptuous and miserable, the Punic and Arab Sicily of Palermo, Trapani, Mozia, Marsala, with noble buildings and magnificent architecture, narrow solemn lanes, vaults and small piazzas, full of sounds and colors that speak a melodious dialect. And there is Eastern Sicily, classic, splendid, melancholy, home to the greatness of the Greek genius and the stagnation of Agrigento, Selinunte, Segesta, Syracuse, Catania, with its harsher and sparer dialect. And lastly the Sicily of the South, of Noto, Modica and Ragusa, of magnificent cathedrals, the "gardens of stone" where the scenic and imaginative Baroque exploded in the land of earthquakes, of fear and rebirth, mourning and light, in an age-old immobility in the land of great baronial landed estates, of an aristocracy, proud untamed "leopards", prisoners of the history that then overwhelmed them.

This artistic multitude, the extraordinary heritage of masterworks and architectural styles that live side by side in Sicily, is one of the miracles of the island, which like few others was capable of receiving

and concentrating different and harmonious models of beauty, of which it goes proud. Its art is the fruit of two thousand eight hundred years of domination, of people who passed here and left traces and evidence of their passage, but also despoiled and abused the land.

History and myth are almost inseparable in Sicily. The spirits of Homer and Ulysses, Demeter and Persephone, Zeus, Apollo and the mythical Elymi, descendants, says Thucydides, of Trojans who survived the war and landed on the western coasts, are ever present. Then came the Phoenicians and the Greeks, the Romans and the Byzantines. After which it was conquered by the Arabs, who reclaimed and loved it, introduced science and oriental knowledge, made it a fertile land and the most flourishing trading center in the Mediterranean. They were followed by the Normans who endowed it with churches and convents and under Frederick II it became the most important court in Europe, the cenacle of illustrious intellects, the melting pot of peoples and religions, the cradle of Italian poetry. After that the Spanish, and the Bourbons, until 1860 when with Giuseppe Garibaldi it became Italian. Paradoxically unification marked the beginning of emigration and impoverishment, and its abandonment by the State penalized it, making its detachment from the continent even more evident.

The Sicilians emerged from this crucible of men, cultures, languages and characteristics of age-old ethnic groups, a proud intelligent people, ceremonious and diffi-

cult, hospitable and withdrawn, contradictory and time-serving, who love to speak in metaphors, with a strong feeling of belonging, a call that follows them wherever they go, as if this land exercised a right and for many of them the return is inevitable. In Quasimodo's words "My land is on the rivers that embrace the sea, no other place has such a slow voice where my feet wander...".

There are blond Sicilians with blue or green eyes and bright cheerful faces, and then there are the dark-haired Sicilians with flashing black eyes, whose faces reflect the tragedy and irony of the ancient Greek

▼ The vermilion Arab domes characterize the silhouette of magic Palermo.

▼ The extravagant Baroque of the churches of Ragusa.

▲ The *Creation of the Stars*, mosaic in the Cathedral of Monreale.

◄▲ The thousand facets of munificent Sicily.

theater or puppet plays. The drama and generosity of this land has given birth to writers and thinkers (some Nobel Prize winners) who made a substantial contribution to the literature of the nineteenth and twentieth centuries, lucidly narrating the primordial land and depth of the Sicilian soul as well as the social condition, as things were, with lucidity and humor.

They say that Sicily is a woman (symbol of the island is the head of a woman), where the goddesses triumphed: Ceres, Aphrodite, Persephone, Arethusa, Diana, are indeed the mythical protagonists. And when Christianity transformed the pagan mythology, it was Mary, the Madonna, ancestral mother and beginning of all human society, to whom the island dwellers turned, worshiping her above all as the sorrowing Mother of Humanity at the foot of the cross where her Son-God and man were sacrificed. This mixture of extremely human tragic and sorrowful religious faith gave rise to the great folkloristic myths that Sicily still tenaciously conserves today and that remain unmistakeably Sicilian.

Sicily, land of wonders, bridgehead between West and East, has been defined as island but not island enough; nation, but not nation enough.

Triangular in shape, Sicily is the largest island in the Mediterranean, surrounded by islands, by the three seas, Tyrrhenian, Ionian and Mediterranean, and with a thousand five hundred kilometers of coastline. Six million inhabitants, concentrated princi-

◄ After the mythical mother goddesses, it is the Madonna who triumphs in this "female" Sicily whose symbol is a woman's head.

pally in Palermo, then in Catania and Messina. An arm of the sea, the strait, only three kilometers wide but deep, is all that separates it from the continent.

Homer in his *Odyssey* called it trinakria (tréis *and* akra): *the land of three promontories, Capo Peloro at Messina, Capo Boeo in Marsala and Capo Passero, while the name Sicily comes from the Indo-European* Sik, *growing in a hurry. For the Romans it was* Triqueta *because of its triangular form and they turned it into a symbol, still used on ceramic decoration: the head of a woman with three legs bent at the knee and set around her face in a ray.*

Even though they live on an island, the Sicilians have continued to be farmers more than fishermen with the exception of the mattanze *of tuna and swordfish, which have become symbols of Sicily. Tourism and related* activities are becoming the most important elements in the economy, with vacationers crowding its islands in summer, and withdrawing in winter to the seductive warmth of aristocratic Taormina, or seeking the snow of Mount Etna, enjoying the cuisine, the pleasures of this land so full of memory, beauty and humanity, kissed by fate and by the gods.

▶▼ The castles and orange groves of this splendid island.

▼ The thousand-colored seas of Sicily.

7

PALERMO

There are places blessed by fate, by beauty and by history. Palermo is one of these. A regal and oriental city of a thousand faces, rich in contrasts and contradictions, where what is real is what appears, but is also its opposite. Palermo is opulent and poor, indolent and effervescent, splendid and melancholy, tender and passionate. But it is also detached and violent, abused and extolled by men and history and always on the verge of death and rebirth, poised between its past and its future. The city has preserved the mystery of bygone things and prides itself in its moving pathetic beauty. The real Palermo initially eludes the visitor, revealing its cosmopolitan and half-caste aspect, inhabited by a people, the Sicilians, generally intelligent, proud, ceremonious and difficult, who speak in metaphors, born from a crucible of characters, of age-old dominating ethnic groups that passed through here.

No other Italian city or region has developed this feeling of "recall", of the law of belonging, as has this land imbued with myth and magic. It is almost as if it were exercising a right that accompanies the inhabitants of Palermo and of Sicily wherever they go, and for many of them returning is inevitable.

Two thousand eight hundred years of foreign rule have left indelible traces in the extraordinary artistic heritage, with masterpieces and architectural styles that co-exist harmoniously: Punic, Greek, Byzantine Palermo; buildings and souks of Arab type; churches and regal Norman castles, fantastic Spanish Baroque up to the twentieth century *art nouveau*.

▼ ▶ The marvelous domes of Palermo and the red domes of the Church of San Giovanni degli Eremiti and its Cloister.

Palermo lies stretched out in the fertile amphitheater-shaped bay at the foot of the bare deserted Mount Pellegrino. Defined by Goethe as "the most beautiful promontory in the world", it is washed by an azure sea with a blue sky that is sometimes tinged with violet, especially when the clammy scirocco, so at home in Palermo, whips in from the desert. Baroque bell towers and glazed scarlet domes mark the profile of the monumental city, the capital of Sicily, the fifth city of Italy with over a million inhabitants (including the hinterland) and with a chaotic

the harmony of some of the districts and the splendid gardens of once upon a time, including the Conca d'Oro or Golden Horn. Even so Palermo, called *Ziz* (flower) by the Carthaginians, maintains its own with a feeling of repressed superiority, and reveals to the unhurried tourist the sublime charm of the historical center, almost a *casbah* with its alleyways, laundry hung on lines, echoing cries, the fatigue of daily living, crumbling ruins of the last war, the reign of cats and dogs, puppeteers, fragrant shops frying *arancini*, *panelle* and bread with the *meusa*; unexpected doorways of once splendid palaces, hiding lovely gardens and magnificent ballrooms worthy of the ancient splendor of a Palermo dominated by a plebeian and refined taste and by a sense of grandeur. Palermo has usually been identified with the mafia, an old phenomenon that plagues the entire island. Today however Palermo is animated by a new fervor of reclamation, thanks also to the economic contributions of Europe, and the aristocracy of Palermo is making a comeback, reopening and giving new life to its palaces. The new illumination enhances the historical center, and plans are underway for a metro to remove some of the traffic from this metropolis, where the old churches and convents are also coming back to life. The symbol of this rebirth is the sixteenth-century roofless

traffic and the typical problems of a large metropolis. The city smells of *zagare* (*zahar*, orange blossom), jasmine and jacarandas that, like the palms, are everywhere, in the parks, along the boulevards, on the terraces. Palermo has made an art of the garden, a concept introduced by the Arabs, who delighted in flowering oases with fountains and plays of water, creating places of delight that recalled Eden. The chronicles of the medieval traveler-geographer Al-Idrisi extolled the beauty of the proverbial gardens of Palermo, rivalling with those of Cordoba, Cairo and the great Baghdad, rose of the East.

While the Normans continued to keep the Saracen gardens of marvels alive, in modern times, above all after World War II, the greed for buildings has in part destroyed

basilica dello Spasimo (a name that recalls the old suffering of this district known as *Kalsa*, from the Arabic *al-Halisah* meaning elect). Now used for exhibitions and cultural venues, a sign of its old ruined state remains in the "*sommacco*", or sumac, a tree that grew by itself in the nave of the basilica.

Palermo also lives by night, in a *movida* that sees the young, and the not so young, as protagonists. Pubs, discotheques, places with music, literary clubs are springing up everywhere, and historical restaurants are once more in business. Waiting for dawn is the rule for many of the night-owl Palermitani. Palermo is also a great city of the sea of which it has

◀ ▲ The typical Via Alloro with glimpses of the sea and a stand selling "*sfincioni*" at Ballarò.

► The roofless Church of Santa Maria dello Spasimo with a sumac tree growing inside.

enting glimpses where least expected. The most splendid views though are from the Foro Italico Umberto I with its palms that almost touch the sea and from those enchanting places Mondello and Addaura.

Since 1624 the Palermitani have venerated the "*Santuzza*" Saint Rosalia, a noble Norman girl, who withdrew to live the life of a hermit in a cave where she died in the flower of her youth. The *Santuzza* saved the city from the plague, and with an incredible display of faith and devotion the people celebrate her for six days every year. Life in the city comes to a halt in this *u festinu*, that achieves its climax on July 15 when the relics of the Saint, enclosed in a silver urn, are carried in procession.

The foundation of Palermo dates to the 8th century B.C. with the Phoenicians, but the Sicani were already there in the third millennium. Then it was conquered by the Greeks, who called it *Panormos* (all port) and for the Carthaginians it became the most important city in the Mediterranean. The Romans conquered and despoiled it in 241 B.C. at the end of the First Punic War and called it *Panormus*. Palermo's golden age began in 831 with its conquest by the Arabs after a year-long siege. They made it one of the most flourishing cities of the time and called it *Balarm*. In 948 it became the capital of the emirate of Sicily. Palermo was transformed into a rich and monumental city, the borders were extended beyond the walls up to the port, which for the first time became the fulcrum for trade in the Mediterranean between Spain and Africa. Three hundred mosques and minarets were built, as well as many other buildings including *hammam* (the baths), scattered throughout the city. The population at the time was two hundred and fifty thousand, but it declined after the expulsion of the Arabs. It has been said that no ruler ever loved Sicily as much as the Arabs during their over a hundred and sixty years on the island, profoundly influencing the language, the taste, the civilization, the cuisine, and teaching that vague, slow and voluptuous way of enjoying and conceiving life that was later inherited by the Normans. The Islamic and Arab culture survived after the expulsion of the Saracens with the Normans of Count Roger de Hauteville who conquered it in 1072, bringing in Christianity and destroying the three hundred mosques in a single night, as told by the historian Ibun Hawqual. His successor Roger II was crowned king of Sicily in 1130 and continued the work of unification. The superb Arab-Norman architectural style, of which the Cathedral of Monreale and the Palatine Chapel are the highest expres-

◄ The monumental Porta Felice seen from the sea.

▲ ▶ Frederick the Great and the wooden *muqarnas* ceiling of the Palatine Chapel decorated with eight-pointed stars, symbolizing the Cosmos.

treatise on the flight of birds of prey and promoted the *School of Sicilian Poetry* which influenced Italian lyric poetry and which Dante mentioned in the *Divine Comedy*. Aragonese dominion lasted up to the 15th century, and was followed by the Spanish who made Palermo a capital of the region: the city became a building site with the construction of palaces, churches, convents, piazzas such as the Quattro Canti and roads, such as Via Maqueda parallel to the old Càssaro, marking the beginnings of Baroque architecture.

sions, was created then. The Normans governed Palermo for a hundred and thirty years and in the words of the historian Denis Mack Smith it was the most opulent period. Frederick II of Swabia, of the Hohenstaufen dynasty, succeeded to the men of the north, and the sovereign-emperor, a man of great stature and intellectual standing, turned the court of Palermo into one of the most cultured in Europe, the cenacle of illustrious minds. He wrote a

At the time Palermo had thirty-eight convents, thirty-nine monasteries, and a hundred and fifty-two churches. The Bourbons arrived in 1734 and were ousted by Garibaldi in 1860 and Palermo and Sicily were annexed to the kingdom of Italy. Palermo once more became a cosmopolitan city and a Mediterranean capital in the *Belle Epoque* with the Florio and the other great industrial families, whose commercial and financial initiatives in the early twentieth

▼ View over the small port of the Cala.

► Piazza Castelnuovo with the Politeama Theater in the background.

century marked the beginning of a period of activity that led to the light-hearted architecture of *art nouveau*: palaces, the **Massimo** and **Politeama** theaters, parks, the **Viale della Libertà** and **Villa Igiea**.

The only way to really understand the city is on foot and the distances are not after all that great. There's a surprise around every corner. Another way of discovering the city is by horse-drawn carriage (opposite the Teatro Massimo), with red velvet cushions and colored plumes, and spend a fabulous hour letting Palermo show you its courtyards and the streets off bounds to cars.

The discovery of Palermo has to begin with that Baroque drawing room called **Piazza Vigliena** or **Quattro Canti** or **Teatro del Sole**; the intersection of the two main thoroughfares, **Corso Vittorio Emanuele** the old **Càssaro** (from the Arabic *el-Qasar*) leading to the sea, at Porta Fe-

lice, and **Via Maqueda** (opened in 1600) dividing the city into four quarters: **Albergheria**, **Kalsa**, **Vucciria**, **Capo**. It is a highly scenic square, with four palaces with three-story concave facades, decorated with figures of animals, statues of the seasons, of the Spanish kings (Charles V, Philip II, III, and IV) and the patron saints of the city (Christina, Agatha, Ninfa and Oliva).

▼ The scenographic Piazza Quattro Canti with its magnificent Baroque palaces.

▲ ▶ The tile dome of San Giuseppe dei Teatini and the sixteenth-century Porta Nuova.

Walking along Corso Vittorio Emanuele on the way to the Norman Palace, in the **Albergheria quarter**, named after the many inns and shelters found there, one comes to the **Church of San Giuseppe dei Teatini** (17th century) with its green and yellow majolica tiled dome. Marble columns separate the two side aisles from the nave in the Latin-cross interior. The splendid frescoes on the dome, supported by eight columns, are by Guglielmo Borremans and Giuseppe Velazquez, while the decorations of the transept vault are by Giuseppe Serpotta.

Porta Nuova, erected in 1583 in memory of Charles V, is at the end of Corso Vittorio Emanuele. The **Palazzo Reale** or **dei Normanni**, now seat of the Sicilian Parliament, faces on the splendid palm gardens of **Villa Bonanno** in **Piazza della Vittoria**. Built in the 11th century by the Emir Assan Ben Alì, it was a fortress with four square towers: the *Greek,* the *Pisan,* the *Joaria* (Arabic for airy), the *Kirimbi.* The only one still standing is the **Pisan Tower.** The Normans enlarged the fort and turned it into a sumptuous palace, whose rooms, according to the historian Ugo Falcando known as the "Sicilian Tacitus" included the harem, the eunuchs' apartments, the throne room as well as others for receptions and prayer and workshops for weaving

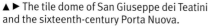

◀ The magnificent palm trees in the park of Villa Bonanno.

▲▼ Piazza della Vittoria with the monument to Philip V and the Palazzo dei Normanni, the Pisan Tower and the interior.

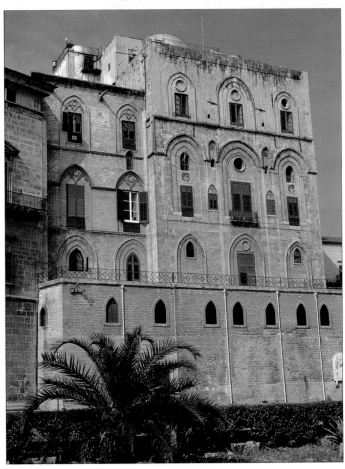

▲ Roger's Room with its splendid mosaic decoration of *Scenes of the hunt* and the Norman *Eagle*.

and embroidering silks. The finest apartments are those of Roger, especially **Roger's Room** on the second floor, a true gem with gold mosaics of scenes of the hunt and stylized trees covering the walls. The **Palatine Chapel** is on the first floor to the right of the loggia of the royal palace and was – in the words of Guy de Maupassant – "the marvel of marvels", an example of that sublime miracle of the fusion of Latin-Byzantine-Arab art produced by Norman and then by Swabian Sicily. Building began for Roger II on Christmas of 1130 and it was consecrated in 1132. It is a basilica, with three apses, the nave and aisles separated by five porphyry columns on each side, with Corinthian capitals, pointed Moorish arches, and a dome. The floor in *pietra dura* mosaic (inlay of semi-precious stone) is Arabian work, the lower parts of the walls are clothed in marble, while the upper parts are covered with mosaics with scenes of the *life of Christ*, and of the *Old Testament*.

◀▶ Detail of the mosaic with the *Baptism of Saint Paul* and view of the apse conch in the Palatine Chapel.

The coffered wooden ceiling (with *muqarnas*) of the nave is entirely decorated with eight-point stars and kufic designs (from *Kufa* ancient Mesopotamian city), the finest monument of Arab art in the world – says the historian Cesare Brandi. The royal throne is covered in *pietra dura* mosaics, and of note is the ambo near the presbytery supported by four columns with next to it a white marble candlestick sup-

▼ ▶ The right aisle and the ambo.

ported by four lions. The mosaic of the blessing *Pantocrator* with his book closed, surrounded by Angels and Archangels is in the vault of the central cupola, while, in the apse conch, is another *Pantocrator* blessing in the Byzantine style.

In front of the entrance on leaving the Palatine Chapel is a curious Indian tree called *Kapor* whose fruits resemble cot-

▼ The typically Islamic decoration with kufic designs on the ceiling of the Palatine Chapel.

► One of the city's cheerful seed stalls and the tile dome of the Church of the Carmine.

ton. There are only three trees of this kind in all Sicily. Taking Via dei Benedettini, to the right of the royal palace, one comes to a monument in Arab style, the former **Church of San Giovanni degli Eremiti**, a cube with five unmistakeable red domes, one for each bay, built by Roger II. The church is entered by passing through the splendid **cloister** with a fine garden of citrus trees, jasmine, pomegranates and prickly pears. Continuing along the lanes and alleys of the Albergheria quarter, after taking a look at the splendid palaces such as **Palazzo Sclàfani**, now military barracks, we are in the heart of the quarter, with the smells, sounds, cries of the crowded *Mercato Ballarò* (from the Arab *al-Bhalharà*), the market with stands selling fish, fruit, meat and the small craft shops. The market continues up to Piazza del Carmine, where the seventeenth-century **Church of the Carmine**, with its majolica dome, stands. Inside is a wooden *Our Lady of Mount Carmel.*

Leaving the stands behind, one comes to the **Church of Gesù** or **Casa Professa**, in the square of the same name, one of the first Jesuit churches in Sicily in a sumptuous Baroque style. Built between 1564 and 1633, it is a glorious riot of colored marbles and intarsias that completely cover it together with stuccoes of angels, cherubs and flowers signed by Giacomo Serpotta.

▼ ► The interior of the domes and the exterior of the Church of San Giovanni degli Eremiti.

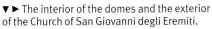

The **Kalsa** is the quarter to the right of Via Maqueda, the old citadel (*al-Halisah*, the elect), Arab fortress where the emir and the administrative officials met. **Piazza Pretoria** is located after the crossroads of the Quattro Canti with at the center the great elliptical Mannerist **fountain** by the Florentine sculptor Francesco Camilliani. Splendidly restored, it is a marvel of white marble, statues, animals, divinities, and monsters. The Palermitani call it the "fountain of shame" because of the nudity of the figures. The **Palazzo Senatorio**, now town hall, with eagles decorating the portal, overlooks the piazza. The **Church of Santa Caterina** (not always open) has a statue of Saint Catherine over the portal. Inside there is another statue of the saint by Gagini. Built between 1580 and 1596, the interior is decorated with stuccoes and marble. Two other churches in Piazza Bellini are La Martorana or dell'Ammiraglio and San Cataldo. **La Martorana** or **Church of Santa Maria dell'Ammiraglio** was named in honor of Eloisa Martorana who founded the nearby convent of Benedictine Sisters (they were the first to make the highly praised *frutta martorana*, of colored marzipan). Greek-cross in plan, the church was built by

▼◄ The Pretoria Fountain (or Fountain of Shame) and detail with the Oreto River.

▲ ► "*Frutta martorana*" and the Churches of La Martorana and of San Cataldo.

George of Antioch, an admiral, in 1143, and renovated in Baroque times. Inside, in the oldest part, are twelfth-century mosaics. A splendid mosaic of Christ Pantocrator surrounded by angels is in the cupola supported by four columns. On the walls are mosaics depicting the *Death of the Virgin*, the *Annunciation* and the *Nativity of Jesus*, and the most popular mosaic, that of *Roger II crowned by Christ*. The small twelfth-century **Church of San Cataldo** is next door. It is in Arab-Norman style with three red domes.

▲ ► Mosaic depicting *Roger II crowned by Christ* and the spell-binding interior of the Church of La Martorana.

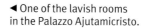

with Baroque rooms that are true masterpieces. It was here that Luchino Visconti shot some of the scenes, including that of the ball, for the film "Il Gattopardo". In the nearby Via Garibaldi one encounters the fine fifteenth-century **Palazzo Ajutamicristo** built by Guglielmo Ajutamicristo and then sold to the Moncada Paternò nobles, a fusion of Gothic-Catalan-Renaissance styles, with a splendid five-arched loggia overlooking the garden of palm and banana trees. Behind the building is one of the loveliest Arab-Norman churches in Palermo,

Other magnificent palaces on Via Maqueda include the **Palazzo Comitini** with frescoed rooms and the fine Baroque eighteenth-century **Palazzo Santa Croce-Sant'Elia** with splendid wrought-iron balconies and railings. Still further on is the eighteenth-century **Palazzo Filangeri di Cutò**. Crossing Via Roma and continuing along Via Lattarini, the old perfume *suq* and the Jewish district, and then a few brothels, while behind the **Church of Sant'Anna** is the astonishing and famous **Palazzo Gangi-Valguarnera**,

the **Church of the Magione** or **Basilica of the Santissima Trinità**, built by Matteo D'Aiello around 1150 for the Cistercian monks. The three-tiered facade is simple and austere, with ogee arches, three windows and three openings. Inside columns and pointed arches separate the side aisles from the nave. An old *Sinopia of Christ* is in the **Sacristy**. The **Cloister** is a masterpiece of elegance: double rows of ogee arches resting on paired columns around a splendidly kept Arab garden.

▼ ► The elegant 12th-century cloister and facade of the Church of the Magione.

▼ ▶ The celebrated Ball Room in Palazzo Gangi, used as setting in the film "The Leopard".

in 1516, calling it the "*Spasimo di Sicilia*" (now in the Prado in Madrid). Crossing Piazza dello Spasimo we are in Via Alloro, a name that means splendid palazzi, and a series of parallel alleys full of smells and picturesque humanity, as in Via IV Aprile where an artisan still makes papier-maché toys, rocking horses and carts. While in Vicolo della Neve, the **Caffè del Parco letterario Tomasi di Lampedusa** not only organizes readings, performances, dedicated to the author of the "Gattopardo" but also serves Sicilian dishes and excellent sweets: one is particularly tempting – a cake called *trionfo della gola* (triumph of gluttony) and never was a name better chosen.

Behind the whole complex of the Spasimo, beyond **Porta Felice** and Via Lincoln, are the **Botanical Gardens** (ten hectares divided into various gardens including a tropical garden with a wilderness of *washingtonia* palms) and **Villa Giulia**, an eighteenth-century garden also known as Flora with the lovely **fountain of the Genio** by Ignazio Marabitti.

Palazzo Abatellis, a sumptuous and elegant late fifteenth-century residence, was built by Matteo Carnelivari for the magistrate Francesco Abatellis. Damaged in the last world war, the palace, restored by the architect Carlo Scarpa, houses the **Galleria Regionale della Sicilia**, a rich museum with works of sculpture and painting of the 14th and 15th century, such as Antonello da Messina's splendid

Behind the Magione is **Santa Maria dello Spasimo**, deconsecrated but now newly restored and used for cultural events. It had cross vaulting but the roof was destroyed in bombings in the last war. It is known as *Spasimo* (suffering) because it was dedicated to the anguish of the Madonna before the Cross, a scene painted by Raphael

▼ ► The *Triumph of Death* and *Crucifix,* by P. Ruzzolone (Galleria Regionale).

► The gigantic banyan tree in the Garibaldi gardens in Piazza Marina.

Virgin Annunciate, and the *Madonna del Latte* by Domenico Gagini, the bust of *Eleonor of Aragon* by Francesco Laurana, and the splendid fresco of the *Triumph of Death* by an unknown painter. There are also fifteenth-century medieval crosses such as the *Crucifix* by Pietro Ruzzolone. Next to the museum are the **Church** (and **Convent**) **of Santa Maria degli Angeli** known as **La Gancia**, of the 16th century. Built as a hospice and shelter for Franciscans, it was then modified. Among the many works it contains of particular interest are the *Madonna with Saints Catherine and Agatha* of 1528 by Antonello da Palermo, and the sixteenth-century *Marriage of Mary* by the sculptor Vincenzo da Pavia. Crossing Via IV Aprile one arrives in the lovely **Piazza Marina** with the Garibaldi gardens, designed by the Sicilian master Ernesto Basile in 1863, and with a gigantic banyan tree. The piazza is lively and full of life evenings as well, with numerous cafes, restaurants and rendezvous, where the best ice cream in Palermo is to be had. Every Sunday there is an antique fair here. In the past it was the arena for executions decreed by the Inquisition, which had its *Sant'Offizio* on the piazza. A number of important buildings face onto the piazza: the seventeenth-century **Palazzo Detti-Fatta**, the **Palazzo Notarbartolo-Greco** of the 18th century, the sixteenth-century **Church of Santa Maria dei Miracoli**, and **Palazzo Chiaramonte** or **Steri**. Begun in 1307 by Manfredi Chiaramonte, a powerful Sicilian feudal family, the splendid building with three floors was restored more than once and in the 15th century was the dwelling of the viceroy and then became the headquarters of the Inquisition in 1601. The palace now houses the university rector's office. The **Puppet Museum** behind contains a collection of over two thousand puppets

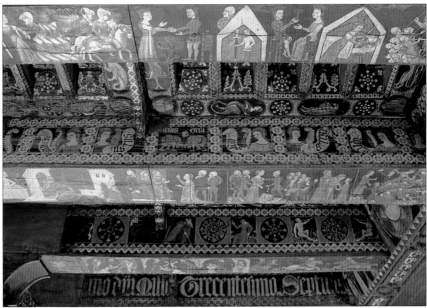

◄ ▼ Palazzo Steri and the Room of the Barons inside.

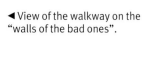

ten statues by Giacomo Serpotta. The church, on the other hand, was founded between 1255 and 1277, restored more than once and bombed in the last war. It still has its fourteenth-century portal and a magnificent rose window. In the fourth chapel on the right is an elegant portal of 1468 by Francesco Laurana, and the entire church has allegorical statues by Giacomo Serpotta, and sculpture by the numerous members of the Gagini family. Back in the Quattro

and marionettes. Nearby, in front of the **Foro Italico Umberto I**, are the **walls** of Palermo called "*le mura delle cattive*" (the walls of the bad ones) because supposedly widows used to promenade there even though they were in mourning. And in front of these, overlooking the sea, is **Palazzo Butera**, where Giuseppe Tomasi di Lampedusa wrote "Il Gattopardo".

Canti, the **Capo** quarter with its colorful *market* is to the left of Corso Vittorio Emanuele. Splendid as an Arabian

The **Church of Santa Maria della Catena**, once near the port, so-named because of the chain that closed the entrance at night, has a fresco of the *Madonna della Misericordia*, statues of *Saints Barbara and Marguerite* by the school of Gagini, and two *sarcophagi*. Returning towards the Quattro Canti, one encounters the **Oratory of San Lorenzo** and the **Church of San Francesco d'Assisi**, the former built in 1569 by the company of Saint Francis with an interior decorated with exuberant stuccoes and

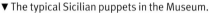

▼ The typical Sicilian puppets in the Museum.

◄ ▼ The Churches of San Francesco and of Santa Maria della Catena.

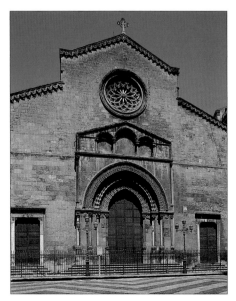

◀ ▲ The *art nouveau* showcase of a bakery at the Capo and the Teatro Massimo.

suq with spices, fruits, vegetables, meat, and fish. Here, as in the other market in Borgo Vecchio, meat is still traditionally roasted in the street, with the *art nouveau* shop windows of the *Morello bakery* serving as backdrop. The **Teatro Massimo**, once more open after being closed for twenty-five years, and the thirteenth-century **Church of Sant'Agostino** with stuccoes by Serpotta and lastly the Cathedral of Palermo are also in this quarter. Dedicated

▼ Bird's-eye view of the Cathedral.

◄ ▲ ▼ The turrets, apses and south flank of the Cathedral.

to the SS. Assunta, the **Cathedral** holds in trust the history and memories of the city. The mortal remains of Constance of Aragon and Henry VI, Frederick II of Swabia and Constance of Hauteville, Peter of Aragon, and Roger II all rest in the sarcophagi inside. Roger's porphyry sarcophagus has figures of Saracens supporting it. The Baroque dome is an eighteenth-century addition, while there are a series of typically Norman crenellations along the right flank. The portico, in magnificent Gothic-Catalan style with three ogee arches and a tympanum with the coats of

▲ Frederick II's red porphyry sarcophagus supported by four lions.

arms of the city, leads to a fifteenth-century portal surmounted by a thirteenth-century mosaic of the *Madonna*. Inside are a wealth of statues by Gagini and Francesco Laurana. To the right of the sanctuary is the **Chapel of Santa Rosalia**, the patron saint, with the finely worked silver reliquary in which her relics are kept. Just as fascinating is the **Chapel of the SS. Sacramento** with the seventeenth-century lapis lazuli ciborium. The **Treasury** is in the **Sacristy**: enamels, goldwork, precious objects found in the tombs, and embroideries, ivories and Byzantine icons. A particularly evocative place is the twelfth-century **Crypt** (newly restored) which contains twenty-three urns, including that of the founder of the Cathedral, Gualtiero Offamilio and the tomb of Frederick of Antioch.

▼ ▶ Silver reliquary of Saint Rosalia and a verse from the Koran in Arab on the side column of the porch.

▲ ▼ View of the nave and the Chapel of San Francesco di Paola.

◀ ▲ The Vucciria market in a painting by Guttuso and as it looks today.

The **Vucciria quarter** to the right of Via Maqueda takes its name from the French *boucherie* or *butcher's shop*, and was celebrated by the Sicilian painter Renato Guttuso. The *vucciria* is not as colorful as it once was, but remains a must for Palermitani and tourists who want to try the *panino con la meusa* (spleen sandwich), and the polyps boiled in the street, but above all to see the masterpieces to be found there: the Convent of San Domenico with the oratory and Santa Zita. The **Convent** and the **Church of San Domenico** with its sumptuous Baroque facade flanked by two bell towers, is surprisingly sober in its decorations. It is the pantheon of the celebrities of Palermo, such as the statesman Francesco Crispi, buried here.

Behind the church in the midst of the market is the **Oratory of the Rosary of San Domenico** with an interior that is a masterpiece in the elegance of the exuberant stuccoes by Serpotta and the allegorical statues of the virtues (signed by him *sirpuzza*). It was built at the end of the 17th century by the Company of the SS. Rosario to which the two artists Serpotta and Gagini belonged. Along the walls are the *Mysteries of the Rosary* painted by Pietro Novelli and Luca Giordano, while a splendid *altarpiece* by Van Dyck dominates the high altar and depicts the *Madonna of the Rosary with the patron saints of the city and Saint Domenic*. Nearby is the other **Oratory of the SS. Rosario of Santa Cita** or **Zita**, a late Renaissance complex built in 1590 and richly decorated inside with stuccoes by Serpotta. It is considered a masterpiece and bears witness to the great achievements of the artist and of Sicilian

◀ ▼ Van Dyck's altarpiece in the Oratory of San Domenico and the *Battle of Lepanto*, by Serpotta, in the Oratory of Santa Cita.

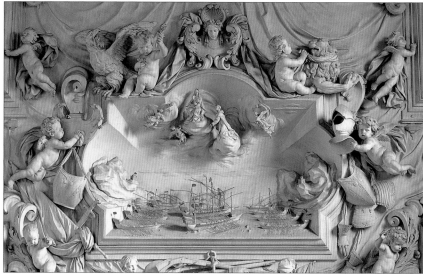

▲ The Oratory of Santa Cita, masterpiece by Giacomo Serpotta.

Baroque. The abundance of cherubs, flowers, garlands, volutes and statues nevertheless seems marvelously light. The *Battle of Lepanto* on the entrance wall is splendid.

The **Museo Archeologico Regionale "Antonino Salinas"** (Via Bara all'Olivella, 24) is in a former eighteenth-century convent. It contains the *metopes* of the temples of Selinunte in addition to sarcophagi and objects that came to light during excavations, including a fragment of a *metope* from Athens' Parthenon.

◄ ▼ The Room of the Selinunte Metopes and *Hercules killing the stag* (Salinas Museum).

There are also various monuments in the outskirts of Palermo that should be seen. For example **La Cuba**, a Fatimite building (signed with an inscription at the top), built in 1180 for William II in the Gonardo Park (now military barracks) was originally surrounded by a large lake. This is where the king came to get away from the torrid heat of the city. In the fourteenth century Giovanni Boccaccio chose it as the setting for one of the short stories in his *Decameron* (V6). **La Zisa**, (from the Arabic *al-aziz* the splendid) built between 1165 and 1167, has a beauty all its own. It resembles La Cuba, rectangular in plan and with a wealth of arches and embrasures. The **Room of the Fountain**, with a cross plan and cross vaulting, *muqarnas* decorations and mosaics of birds on the walls, is quite lovely. **San Giovanni dei Lebbrosi** is one of the oldest Arab-Norman monuments, dating to 1071, with its red domes and pointed arches. The church stands in a fine palm garden. The **Catacombs of the Capuchin Monks** are macabre but haunting. They are in a cemetery annexed to the church with eight thousand mummified bodies, some dressed in elegant clothing, the remains of religious figures and the wealthy of Palermo. Ippolito Pindemonte mentions them in the sepulchral poem that was never finished and Guy de Mau-

The Room of the Fountain in La Zisa and the old Church of San Giovanni dei Lebbrosi.

▲▼ View of the orientalizing Chinese Palace and the splendid Italian-style gardens.

passant felt ill when he saw them. The **Chinese Palace** on the other hand, a gay structure with orientalizing motifs and completely frescoed, was built in 1799 by Venanzio Marvuglia for Ferdinand I of Sicily and Maria Carolina in the **Park of la Favorita**, the green lung of Palermo with its four hundred hectares of park. The **Museo Etnografico Pitré**, also located here, has an important collection of artefacts connected with Sicilian folklore.

▲ ► Mount Pellegrino, the grotto of Saint Rosalia and the statue of the Saint.

The **Shrine of Santa Rosalia**, the patron saint of Palermo and a pilgrim site, is on **Monte Pellegrino**. It is located next to the convent, inside a grotto where the Saint withdrew as a hermit and died young in 1166. According to tradition Saint Rosalia, born in 1130, was the daughter of the Norman noble Sinibaldo, related to William II.

In 1624 she appeared to a fisherman to reveal where her bones were. When they were carried to Palermo, the city was liberated from the plague. After this miracle the *Santuzza* as she is called became the patron saint of the city and in addition to the six-day *festinu* every July, she is celebrated on September 4 with the *acchianata*, the pilgrimage to the grotto.

The holiday resort of **MONDELLO**, with the "Charleston", an *art nouveau* bathing establishment, is a favorite with the Palermo beach goers.

About a dozen kilometers from Palermo is **PIANA DEGLI ALBANESI**, a curious town inhabited from the 15th century on by a group of Albanians who had moved

◄ Costumes on show
for the feast of the *Santuzza*.

▲ The splendid bay of Mondello.

here after the Turko-Ottoman invasion (others arrived during the war in 1941). The six thousand inhabitants here speak their own language, the religion is Greek Orthodox and the street signs are bilingual. It is worth a visit for the spectacular liturgical ceremonies in traditional costumes, such as the *feast of January 6* with the immersion of the Cross recalling the baptism of Christ, or the *feast of the patron saint Maria Odigitria* or for the rites of the Holy Week that attract hosts of tourists.

A few kilometers from Piana degli Albanesi, is **CORLEONE** a town of Arab origins, and a name well-known to the American public thanks to the cinema.

▼ ▶ Traditional costumes and Greek Orthodox liturgy at Piana degli Albanesi.

MONREALE

Monreale is a small town on a hill eight kilometers from Palermo and easy to reach by bus. The panorama from this terrace over Palermo, the sea and the Conca d'Oro (no longer a valley of orange groves but of cement) is extraordinary. Monreale has only a few streets, two small squares with souvenir shops, coffee and pastry shops, trattorias, butcher shops still called *carnezzeria*, and then the Cathedral, one of the most beautiful examples of religious architecture in the world, a masterpiece of Byzantine-Arab-Norman art. The **Cathedral** of Monreale, built for William II known as the Good – who spared no expenses, as expression of the power of the Normans – was begun in 1172 and finished barely ten years later. It was dedicated to Mary and entrusted to the order of Benedictine monks for whom an abbey was also built.

▲ Panorama of Monreale, the Conca d'Oro and Palermo from Mount Caputo.

▼ The facade of the Cathedral of Monreale.

▲ ▼ Details of the mosaic of the *Creation* and *Willialm II offering the Madonna a model of the Cathedral*.

An eighteenth-century **portico** with three arches and a tower at each end constitutes the facade. Entry is through the bronze "**doors of paradise**", designed by Bonanno da Pisa in 1186, with *episodes from the Bible* and with the *lion* and the *griffin*, symbols of the Normans, below. The glittering golden interior is breath-taking. Columns with Roman capitals and pointed arches separate the side aisles from the nave in this Latin-cross structure. The floor is in marble mosaic and the wooden ceiling is decorated. The church is completely covered by six thousand one hundred and forty square meters of brightly colored **mosaics** made in the 12th and 13th centuries by Byzantine, Arab and Venetian craftsmen. They depict the stories of the *Old and New Testament*, in the nave, and the *Acts of the Apostles*, and the *Gospels*, in the aisles and the walls of the apses. The mosaics culminate in the *Christ Pantocrator* who dominates the church from the apse conch on high. He is shown blessing in the Greek manner, with an open book in his other hand. Just as beautiful are the mosaics of the *Madonna Odigitria* (she who indicates the way), those of the *Creation*, with birds and fish, and two that show *King William II dressed as basileus*, that is king, *giving a model of the Cathedral to the Madonna*, and that of the *king crowned by Jesus Christ*. The mortal remains

▲ ▼ Detail of one of the capitals in the Cathedral and the eastern apse.

of William I and his mother, of William II and his wife Marguerite of Navarre repose inside the Cathedral. The three splendid and monumental **apses**, facing east, decorated with a play of interlacing pointed arches and rosettes with inlays in marble and tufa, masterpiece of Norman art, can be seen best upon leaving the church, right behind Vicolo dell'Angelo. The elegant **cloister** of the Benedictine

▲ ▼ The cloister and small cloister of the Benedictine abbey and detail of one of the 228 capitals.

abbey presents a series of pointed arches supported by 228 paired columns with mosaic encrusted shafts, all different, with splendid carved capitals. In a corner is a **small cloister** enclosing a fountain in the shape of a stylized palm tree.

Around ten kilometers from Monreale, among the pines, is the **Monastery of San Martino delle Scale**, dating to the 14th century, built on the remains of the old Monastery founded by St. Gregory the Great. It contains frescoes by Pietro Novelli.

Words and the Island

▲ Vitaliano Brancati

▲ Giovanni Verga and Federico De Roberto

Without the Sicilian writers and poets, Italian literature, one of the most noble and oldest in the European spirit, would not be nearly as rich as it is. Sicilian poetry was the first to be based on the vernacular rather than on Latin (thirteenth century) and from the late nineteenth century to the present the works of great authors have gone well beyond the confines of the island and of Italy. Two of them, Luigi Pirandello and Salvatore Quasimodo, were also the recipients of the Nobel Prize for Literature (respectively 1943 and 1959). They were preceded towards the end of the 19th century by other writers whose novels are still being read, by Giovanni Verga who wrote of the hard life and destiny of the fishermen and sulphur miners in his "I Malavoglia" (Under the Medlar Tree) and "Mastro Don Gesualdo", and by Federico De Roberto who realistically depicted the superstitions of the decadent Sicilian aristocracy in "The Viceroys".

▲ Luigi Capuana

▲ Luigi Pirandello and Marta Abba

Luigi Pirandello with his subtle logic and extraordinary feel for drama is considered one of the greatest playwrights of twentieth century Europe. "Sei personaggi in cerca di autore" (Six characters in search of an author), Henry IV, "Come tu mi vuoi", "Così è se vi pare" (That's How it Is, if You like) continue to be performed throughout the world, illustrating the existential and social crisis of modern man.

Sicily also produced great novels, especially in the twentieth century. Examples are Pirandello's "Il fu Mattia Pascal" (The Late Mattia Pascal), "Uno, nessuno e centomila". After World War II Elio Vittorini ("Conversations in Sicily") inaugurated epic literature of the "humiliated man". The Catanian Vitaliano Brancati ironically and proudly portrayed the vices of the Sicilian bourgeoisie and their so-called sexual conceits. Giuseppe Tomasi di Lampedusa painted a picture of the funereal and genial decadence of the Sicilian aristocracy in the middle of the 19th century in his novel "Il Gattopardo" (The Leopard), later turned into a film by Luchino Visconti. Leonardo Sciascia from Racalmuto was another great contemporary writer, gifted with an acute social sense and ingenious judicial fantasy. His novels "Il giorno della civetta" (The Day of the Owl), "Todomodo" (One Way or Another), "Gli zii di Sicilia" (Sicilian Uncles), present us with a raw cross-section of the mafia, justice and Sicilian society. Currently, next to novelists such as Gesualdo Bufalino ("Diceria dell'untore" or The Plague Sower) and Vincenzo Consolo, the television version of Andrea Camilleri's detective novels involving the police superintendent Montalbano have become particularly popular.

▲ Elio Vittorini

▲ Leonardo Sciascia

The Sicilian poets of today include the populist Ignazio Buttitta, who gives voice in dialect to the Sicilians without a voice, and Salvatore Quasimodo, who received the Nobel Prize in the 1950s, a mythical poet of Sicily's Greek nature (and a great translator of the ancient Greek Lyrics) and, later, of the human condition of modern man oppressed by contemporary power and violence ("Ed è subito sera", "La terra impareggiabile" or The Incomparable Earth and "La vita non è un sogno" or Life is not a Dream).

▲ Giuseppe Tomasi di Lampedusa

▲ Salvatore Quasimodo

BAGHERIA

O n the sea, surrounded by citrus groves, orchards and olive trees is Bagheria "with that air of a summer garden" as Dacia Maraini, who was born here, describes it in her book of the same name. Bagheria in the eighteenth century was where the wealthy aristocrats of Palermo and Sicily built their Baroque villas, among the most luxurious on the island.

Today Bagheria is not much more than a satellite of Palermo, fourteen kilometers from the capital and suffocated by cement. The overwhelming fragrance of the *zagara* and the salt-laden air still succeed in making these superb villas a bit less melancholy. It was here that the painter Renato Guttuso was born in the twentieth century, and the poet Ignazio Buttitta, bard of Sicily, and the film director Giuseppe Tornatore.

The eighteenth-century **Villa Palagonia** of Prince Francesco Gravina di Palagonia is one of the most celebrated with its fantastic tufa *figures of giants* and *mytho-*

▲ ▼ The entrances to the Baroque Villa Palagonia in Bagheria.

logical monsters. The villa was built in an elliptical form enlivened by a play of staircases and balconies by the eccentric architect Tommaso Maria Napoli. In 1721 the same architect built the equally exuberant **Villa**

▲ ◄ Close-ups of anthropomorphic figures decorating Villa Palagonia.

Valguarnera, with a setback facade and a staircase with sculptures by Ignazio Marabitti. The villa is surrounded by a park and by citrus groves; from the windows one can see the sea. **Villa Butera**, the oldest, dates to 1658 but was renovated in the 18th century. The **Gallery of Modern Art**, with a fine collection of paintings by Renato Guttuso, is located in the imposing eighteenth-century **Villa Cattolica**, also with two parallel staircases.

▲ The lavish Hall of Mirrors of Villa Palagonia.

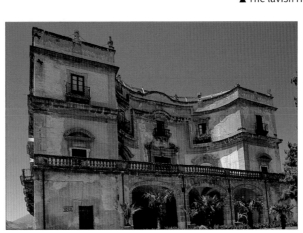

► The facade of Villa Cattolica, premises of the Gallery of Modern Art with works by Renato Guttuso.

▲ ▶ The archaeological site of Solunto and remains of the columns of the Gymnasium.

Three kilometers separate Bagheria from the Punic *Soloeis*, today **SOLUNTO**, an interesting Greco-Roman archaeological site on the slopes of Mount Catalfano from which there is a fine panorama of the sea. What is left today are the ruins of a **Gymnasium**, with the solitary Doric columns, part of the trabeation, cisterns for water, the

tiers and the scena of a Hellenistic **Theater** and the **House of Leda**, with a mosaic floor. The finds (excavations are still in progress) are in the **Antiquarium** at the entrance to the site as well as in the Museum in Palermo.

◀ Statue and theater mask found during the excavations (Antiquarium).

CEFALÙ

Cefalù is one of the most charming cities in Sicily, a lively seaside resort on the Tyrrhenian coast with a beach of fine sand, popular in summer and with a small picturesque fishing port. It is located in a bay between the Tyrrhenian sea and the Rocca dominated by the imposing Cathedral around which it grew.

▼ ► Splendid Cefalù and its bay.

the other, from one window to the next, has never died down. The houses and streets along the waterfront on the other hand are modern and rectilinear, full of shops, restaurants and cabarets. A delightful souvenir of Cefalù are the hot water bottles in ceramic, copying the old ones called *Mariteddu* because their warmth was a substitute for that of absent husbands.

The **Cathedral** is Cefalù's most important Arab-Norman monument. It was built in 1131 for Roger II in fulfilment of a vow. Like a fortress, the facade has various tiers and is framed by two massive bell towers. The portico, a fifteenth-century addition, consists of three arches, two pointed and one round, supported by four columns and with ribbed vaulting, sheltering the magnificent portal, **Porta Regum**, with marble carving. The church is beautiful and architecturally

The medieval historical center consists of a labyrinth of alleyways, courtyards, stairways that crisscross, with the tangle of houses almost touching each other in some corners of the town and where the art of *curtigghiu*, gossiping about everything and everybody from one balcony to

▲ *Portrait of an Unknown Man*
by Antonello da Messina
(Mandralisca Museum).

▲ ▼ The sea of Cefalù seen from its small harbor and
the Rocca and the ruins of the Temple of Diana.

harmonious, as are the golden **mosaics** that cover the apse and half of the side walls, the work of Byzantine and Arab craftsmen. The image of the blessing *Christ Pantocrator*, holding the book, looks down from the apse conch. Below him, at the center, is the *Madonna*, with on either side the four *Archangels* clothed in Byzantine style. On the lower levels *Saints, Prophets* and *Apostles*. Numerous statues adorn the Cathedral. Of particular note are a *Madonna and Child* by Antonello Gagini in the transept while the artist of the smiling *Madonna and Child* of the 14th century in the Chapel of the SS. Sacramento is unknown. The *wooden Christ* of 1468 is by Guglielmo da Pesaro and there is a Romanesque *baptismal font* in the right aisle.

Opposite the Cathedral is the **Mandralisca Museum** with its remarkable collection, in particular Antonello da Messina's *Portrait of an Unknown Man*. The ruins of the fourteenth-century **Osterium Magnum**, Roger's royal residence with its original three- and two-light windows, are in Via Ruggero.

For a spectacular panorama from the top of the **Rocca**, you need good legs and an hour's climb. Then the remains of the **Temple of Diana**, 9th century B.C., on which the Greeks built another temple in the 5th- 4th century B.C., can also be visited.

ISLAND OF USTICA

▲ The crystal clear waters of Punta Arpa.

Ustica is a tiny volcanic island in the shape of a turtle. It is the oldest of the Aeolian Islands and two hours by ferry from Palermo. The Romans called it *Ustum* (burnt) on account of its black earth, but it was always fertile and ideal for growing crops of all kinds, particularly lentils, the pride of its thousand inhabitants.

Ustica: from an island of sorrowful exile, where those who opposed the Bourbons and later the Fascist government were confined, to a dream island, with limpid waters thanks to the Atlantic currents, and some of the finest underwater flora in the Mediterranean, fields of poseidonia oceanica, red gorgonians, sponges of all kinds such as the famous *elephant ears*. The depths of Ustica are also an archaeological park where Greek and Punic amphoras lie at rest, shipwrecked Roman ships and Saracen finds. The coastline is deeply indented, with cliffs that drop sheer to the sea, hiding magnificent coves and grottoes, such as the **Grotta Azzurra** or **Blue Grotto** named after the color of the water, the **Grotta della Pastizza**, **Punta Galera**, and **Punta Cavazzi** with its natural green pool between two enormous rocks that communicate with the sea through a cleft.

In 1987 the Region of Sicily instituted the nature reserve with a *Marine National Park*, the first in Sicily, to safeguard the flora and fauna as well as the barracuda, tuna and swordfish. But Ustica is also the island of migrating birds and bird watchers too flock here in the periods of migration.

The only town on the island is also called **Ustica**, the houses painted with colorful *murales* crowded around the small port of **Santa Maria**. A climb up a staircase with amaranth and red hibiscus flowers leads to the center with three small squares, one after the other, the church and the **Archaeological Museum** with finds of the 15th century B.C. of the *prehistoric village* at I Faraglioni.

▼ ► The colorful "murales" of Ustica and the prehistoric village at I Faraglioni.

SEGESTA

Segesta with its superb age-old temples, custodians of the ancient Greco-Siciliote civilization, is located near Mount Barbaro, behind the gulf of Castellamare. The isolated archaeological park overlooks a melancholy landscape of bare hills.

All that remains of what was once a glorious and powerful city with an enormous busy harbor is a Doric temple, a theater, stones and a few ruins found in recent excavations. It was an ally of Athens and dear to its founders, the Elymi, the mysterious people of the 8th century B.C., perhaps descendents of the Trojans who had fled from the Achaeans and joined the Sicani, native to the site. Traditionally the name Segesta comes from a Trojan nymph who welcomed and protected Aeneas when he landed in Sicily.

Segesta became even more beautiful and powerful with the Greeks: the city was permeated with Greek culture, customs and civilization. It had its own coinage and traded with the Mediterranean countries. The Carthaginians who destroyed Selinunte in 409 B.C. settled in Segesta. Under Roman rule it was *libera et immunis* or a free and exempt city and the economy flourished. Segesta's history stopped in the Middle Ages with the arrival in A.D. 486 of the Vandals who sacked the city and razed it to the ground, but did not dare to violate the temples and the theater. The **Temple** in all its majesty stands alone on a bare hill, built in Doric style, a blend of severity and proportion, when the city was at its zenith. To stand in front of this temple, one of the best preserved of classic Sicily, is a particularly poignant moment. There are fourteen columns on the long sides, six on the facade and back. They are nine meters high and two meters in diameter.

Some believe it was never finished, perhaps due to the war. Others say that the absence of the covering made it possible to celebrate sacrificial and sacred rites at the center, in the open air.

▼ The majestic and solitary Temple of Segesta (430-420 B.C.)

The **Theater** is located further north, within the walls where the acropolis was, overlooking the hills and sea of Castellamare in the distance. Dating to the 3rd century B.C., it follows the design of Greek amphitheaters. The **cavea** is dug out of the slope of the hill, a hemicycle sixty-three meters in diameter. There are twenty tiers of stone seats, subdivided into seven sectors. The **orchestra**, where the choir was located, is eighteen meters

in diameter and with extraordinary acoustics. The theater could seat up to four thousand spectators and still today, in the long summer nights, rings with the ancient magic of Greek and Latin tragedies.

Leaving Segesta for a visit to **CALATAFIMI**, the old Arab hamlet, one passes the famous *Terme Segestane* or baths where Heracles, comforted and refreshed by the nymphs, bathed in the waters they brought forth. The

hot springs gush out on the banks of the river Caldo and inside a grotto form a pool-sauna with a temperature of thirty-eight degrees C. The Romans appreciated the therapeutic properties and were frequent visitors. *Qalat al Fim*, now Calatafimi-Segesta, surrounded by cork oak woods and Mediterranean maquis, is the town the Arabs built only four kilometers away when Segesta fell into oblivion after being sacked by the Vandals. The Muslims founded it around the old Byzantine fortress of Eufemio on the slopes of the hill.

It became part of Italian history in 1860 as the site of the battle where Garibaldi's Thousand under his command defeated the Bourbon army, opening the way to Palermo and the conquest of the island.

At the center of the town is the **Chiesa Madre**, medieval in its origins but enlarged in the 16th century. Of partic-

ular note in the three-aisled interior is the lovely *Madonna and Child with Saints* on the altar, attributed to the sculptor Bartolomeo Berrettaro.

Calatafimi is at its liveliest for the ***Festa del Crocifisso*** held every five years from May 1 to 3. The many processions are accompanied by allegorical floats with living tableaux, an extraordinary mixture of faith, tradition, and folklore.

ALCAMO, not far from Calatafimi, is a town surrounded by a splendid countryside of age-old Saracen olive groves and vineyards. It has always produced an excellent *doc* wine known as *bianco d'Alcamo*, with a fresh, dry, fruited flavor.

Alcamo was founded by the Arabs and was named after the founder *Manzil Alqamah*. This is the birthplace of the illustrious poet Cielo d'Alcamo who wrote one of the oldest texts in the vernacular "*Rosa fresca aulentissima*", also cited by Dante, in the thirteenth century. Of interest in Alcamo are the **castle of the Counts of Modica** of the 14th century with two cylindrical and two square towers and the fourteenth-century **Chiesa Madre della Madonna dell'Assunta**, rebuilt in subsequent centuries and flanked by a bell tower. The three chapels inside contain sculpture by Gagini and frescoes by Borremans and Giuseppe Renda of Alcamo.

▼ ▶ The castle of the Counts of Modica in Alcamo and the vineyards.

"Qui si fa l'Italia o si muore"

At half past one on May 11, 1860 Giuseppe Garibaldi landed in the harbor of Marsala, strangely unguarded, with 1089 men, of which fifty were Sicilian, and a single woman, Francesco Crispi's companion who, as a fervid patriot, cooked for the soldiers.

Marsala was an English colony, inhabited by numerous merchants and wine producers who welcomed Garibaldi and his red-shirted volunteer army, burning with enthusiasm and patriotic love. Their famous red shirts lent them the passion and fire they needed to succeed in the practically impossible undertaking of driving out the Bourbon army and finally uniting all of Italy under a single banner.

Four days after the landing, Garibaldi won the battle of Calatafimi with the cry of "*qui si fa l'Italia o si muore*" (here we'll make Italy or die), opening the way to Palermo. For the occasion he had named his white horse "Marsala".

Garibaldi was neither a politician nor an intellectual. He was a man of action, plain-spoken and fiery, a sailor who had become a professional revolutionary. Considered "the folk hero of two worlds" he had fought at length and successfully in Latin America. Still today, a century and a half later, he continues to be a legendary symbol of those who fight for justice and liberty.

After the victory of Calatafimi, in which he was wounded, in Marsala Garibaldi accepted the office of "dictator of Sicily" for Victor Emmanuel II, king of Sardinia and Piedmont. As dictator he prohibited sacking and robbing, under threat of the firing squad.

The battle for the liberation of Palermo was difficult because the troops of General Lanza were armed and well equipped, unlike Garibaldi's volunteers. Great captain that he was, he attempted to surprise the enemy by fooling them into believing that he was in the Sicilian hinterland while he was actually only twenty-three kilometers from Palermo. An English journalist who met him in a hut observed that he had a small barrel of marsala wine with him. The firm of Florio, where our hero had tasted the wine, later called one of its wines *Marsala Garibaldi dolce* in his honor.

Garibaldi's troops entered Palermo at two o'clock in the morning on May 27 and fought for eight hours, defeating the Bourbons.

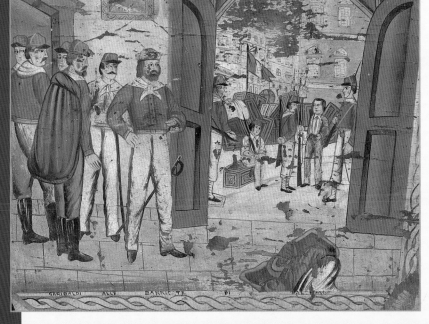

▲ Ossuary Monument at Pianto Romano, by Ernesto Basile.

Garibaldi's contribution to the Italian Risorgimento was more than military. He knew how to trigger the revolution from the lower ranks and this contributed even more to dissension with Count Camillo di Cavour, who was not overly enthusiastic of his successes.

In the midst of prickly pears, cactus and cane-brakes, the Bourbons were definitively defeated on July 20, 1860 at Milazzo and driven from the island. Two hundred Garibaldini died. Garibaldi's advance into continental Italy was brought to a halt by General La Marmora (because of regional politics) to whom the leader replied with the famous phrase "*obbedisco*".

◄ *Garibaldi and the Garibaldini* on the side of a Sicilian cart.

SAN VITO LO CAPO

◀ ▲ Preparation of a seafood couscous, a typical local dish.

The old marine hamlet of San Vito Lo Capo with three thousand inhabitants lies at the base of the promontory of Monte Monaco in a bay washed by a clear, crystalline blue sea and with a beach of crushed shells. It is a proverbial marvel.

The international popularity of San Vito Lo Capo depends on the many cultural and food and wine events that rotate around the *Cous Cous Fest* where every August world-renowned cooks vie with each other in preparing couscous, a symbolic dish of the integration of diverse civilizations, peoples and cultures.

The hamlet of San Vito embraces the old Arab fortress that was transformed in the 13th century into the Shrine of San Vito and summer evenings serves as venue for performances and concerts.

The *Riserva Naturale dello Zingaro*, seven kilometers of protected coastline (walkable) with *faraglioni*, bays, coves, one after the other, kissed by the waves and with a flourishing Mediterranean vegetation, separates San Vito Lo Capo from Scopello (called *Scopelos* or shoals by the

▼ The lovely coast of the Riserva Naturale dello Zingaro.

baglio or Sicilian stronghold that was once the *bahal* (courtyard) of an Arab farmhouse. A piazza, an old stone watering trough and a few paved lanes and alleys are the historical center.

Sheltered by a cavern on the coast, in sight of an old tower, the **Tonnara di Scopello** dates to 1200 and belonged to Frederick II as shown by documents on exhibit inside. It was used up to a few years ago, and today is a small **Museum** in which all the equipment and tools used in tuna fishing can be seen. The abundance of tuna in this sea led the Greeks, who knew it well, to call it *Cetaria*, "land of the tuna".

Greeks), the other resort town with its splendid *Baia di Guidaloca*, with white pebbles. This and the small coves face onto the shoreline of sheer rocks, while the sea is dominated by the imposing *faraglioni* or reefs.

SCOPELLO is enveloped in a blinding light, a transparent green-blue sea, surrounded by dwarf palms and a Mediterranean maquis or *macchia* fragrant with eucalyptus, broom (*ginestra cinera*) and wild plants. This unsullied strip of land is indeed a corner of paradise. Scopello Alto, the hamlet, overlooks the coast from its a hundred and six meters of altitude on Mount Sparagio, with the houses backed up against a seventeenth-century

▼ The imposing "*faraglioni*" or stacks at Scopello.

▲ ▼ Small beach of the Zingaro sanctuary at Scopello and the dwarf palm that grows wild here.

ERICE

A steep winding road leads to Erice, with a breathtaking panorama. The town is perched on the top of Mount San Giuliano at an altitude of seven hundred and fifty meters, opposite Trapani, and the Egadi Islands. On a clear day Africa looks close. Erice counts thirty thousand inhabitants and has always been a resort, especially for the bourgeoisie of Trapani.

This charming town is really worth a visit (with good walking shoes). It is a real medieval gem, triangular in shape with three entrances: **Porta Spada**, **Porta Trapani** and **Porta del Carmine**, and is surrounded by imposing walls.

▲▼ Porta Spada and the Punic walls and panorama of the city.

Stone is the most striking element in this citadel: the many churches, the Arab-Norman houses with their loggias, courtyards and patios adorned with plants and flowers, are all in stone. The piazzas of Erice are narrow, the labyrinth of paved lanes and alleyways wind continuously up and down. The *vanelle*, small corridors where one has to pass one at a time, built by the Arabs for defense, are also in stone.

▲ ▲ Streets and charming views of medieval Erice.

Erice today is visited by hosts of foreigners and tourism may be the most important element in its economy. In 1963 the *Istituto Scientifico Ettore Majorana* was founded in the old monastery of San Pietro and scholars and visitors come for meetings from every part of the world. In antiquity the king of Erice is said to have had a temple built on the Olympus of the city dedicated to the cult of his mother, goddess of love, beauty and fertility. Thus Erice became a sacred city, the most important religious center in Sicily and the Mediterranean. Mythology aside, Erice was a Carthaginian colony up to 260 B.C. and when the Romans took over in 241 B.C. it was despoiled of all its riches. The Arabs called it *Ghebel-Hamed*. When it was conquered in the 12th century by the Norman Roger II the city flourished anew.

Today, in addition to tourism, Erice produces and exports finely decorated ceramics and still makes lovely cotton rugs and throws in the old *frazzata* technique, with recycled textiles woven in colorful geometric patterns. The town also has its tradition in sweets with excellent pastries in marzipan, *pasta reale*, spiced chocolate, ricotta prepared with recipes of the convent. A pause in the old *Pasticceria del Convento*, in the center, is a must for its famous cocoa *biscotti pallini* or the *dolci di Badia* with marzi-

▼ ▶ The typical *frazzate* or rag rugs of the city.

pan and lemon cream, a true delight for gourmets. From late April to the middle of May – for the *festival of the ginestra* with the fragrant yellow flowers of broom heralding summer – Erice makes a show of its crafts and sweets. The houses are all decorated with *ginestra* and the entire city is redolent and yellow. Erice has been called the small Sicilian Switzerland. **Corso Vittorio Emanuele**, the old Via Regia, is the main street that begins at Porta Trapani. It is the street for shopping, cafes, lovely patrician palaces and souvenir shops. The **Chiesa Matrice**, dedicated to the Madonna, was built in stone in 1314 by king Frederick II of Aragon and still has its superb porch. Next to it is the massive detached bell tower with two-light

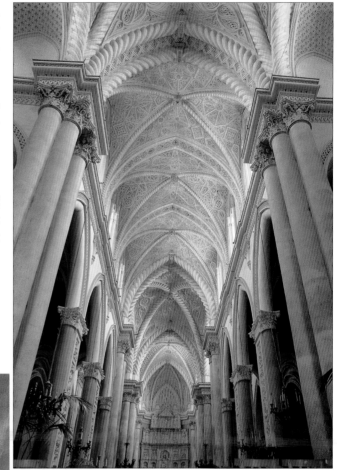

▼ ► The Cathedral of Erice with the bell tower and view of the nave.

openings, originally a watch tower. The church has a nave and side aisles and a lovely fifteenth-century *Madonna and Child*, a sculpture of Sicilian school by Domenico Gagini. A work in marble by Antonello Gagini is the *Annuncia-*

▼ The typical sweets of Erice.

◄ ▲ The *Madonna of the Pears*, 18th century,
in the Church of San Giovanni Battista and the Castle
rebuilt by the Normans on the ruins of the Temple of Venus.

tion, to be seen in the nearby **Cordici Museum** (Palazzo del Municipio), right at the entrance.

Not far from the museum are the **Churches of San Martino** and of **San Giuliano**. The former, of Norman origins was restructured in 1600 and has noteworthy wooden *choir stalls*. Adjacent to the church is the **Oratory of the Congretion of Purgatory** in pure rococo style. The **Church of San Giuliano**, painted pink, Norman but restored in the 17th century, was frequently renovated and is today used as a cultural center. Fine works in the church of **San Giovanni Battista** include a statue of *Saint John the Baptist* by Antonino Gagini and a *Saint John Evangelist* by Antonello Gagini, Domenico's son, as well as some fourteenth-century frescoes.

Climbing up to the ancient **Acropolis**, the site of the *Temple of Venus Erycina*, is the imposing **Castle of Venus**, rebuilt by the Normans on the remains of the antique temple. Inside is a sacred well, ruins of the old temple, the remains of a Carthaginian house and a Roman bath. Nearby, in the midst of a nineteenth-century public park, is the **Castello Pepoli** or **Balio** with its tower, symbol of Erice. It was once the headquarters of the *Baiuolo* governor.

▼ ► *Small head of Aphrodite*
(Cordici Museum), the Castle and
the Balio Tower, symbol of Erice.

SALT AND SALTPANS

S un and wind, said the ancients "*fanno lu salinaiu cuntentu*". For salt one needs sea water, a hot sun, wind and the work of the *salinaio* or salter.

Sicily is rich in salt-works. They are scattered throughout the provinces, and some as in Syracuse are no longer in use while those of the area of Trapani, and of Pachino, Cantoni, Moranella, work full pace.

The saltpans in the **Riserva Naturale di Trapani** extend over an area of nine hundred fifty hectares and in recent years have produced one hundred and ten thousand tons of salt that arrives on the tables of the entire world. Sicilian salt is special, rich in potassium and magnesium, and with a low percentage of sodium. It is highly soluble and sought after for the preservation of foodstuffs.

The coastal road that leads from Trapani to Marsala crosses the Riserva and is known as the "*via del sale*" or salt route. The landscape is unreal, a vast plain with windmills, white conical pyramids of salt glittering in the sun by day and turning scarlet, ruby and amaranth at sunset.

It is said that the first to install pans for the extraction of salt were the Phoenicians. With Frederic II they became a Crown monopoly, in other words royal property.

Since 1500 the port of Trapani has been one of the most important in Europe for the exporting of salt, as precious as gold in trading merchandise. The crisis in the Sicilian salt-works came with the Unification of Italy and the creation of salt-works in Sardinia.

▲▼ A marvelous sunset reflected in the saltpans and the windmill that characterizes the landscape.

Recently the **Salt Museum** has been instituted in Nubia (Arab name for gold), five kilometers from Trapani, in a 17th century *baglio*. Here the tools used in extracting salt are on exhibit.

▲ Piles of salt and the saltpans.

The baskets of salt the *salinai* used to carry on their backs have given way to conveyer belts, and the windmills now run on diesel fuel. The meter-high walls that separated the basins and formed checkerboard patterns, are still in the tufa of the Egadi Islands, while the terracotta tiles protecting the piles of salt are still the old hand-made ones.

The different shapes and depths of the saltpans hastened evaporation, leaving the salt on the bottom. Dutch windmills were used to transfer the saline water from one pan to the next, through a system of canals and locks.

The first basins for the incoming sea water were called *fridda*, after which came the *cruda* or *retrocalda* followed by the *vasi cultivu*, pans in which it blends with the yeast-like residue deposited by previous cultures. After various other passages the water ends in the *caseddri* where the layers of pure salt crystals form.

◀▼ Interior and exterior of the Salt Museum in Nubia.

TRAPANI

Trapani is a special town, stretched out on a promontory where the waters of the Tyrrhenian and the Mediterranean mingle, the extreme point of western Sicily. It is a city unlike the other Sicilian cities: it is ancient but has a Baroque soul. Bombed in the last war it now looks modern, but is not anonymous despite the fact that much of its historical heritage was lost. There are splendid convents, churches, palaces and patrician residences with opulent facades next to ruined portals, and the narrow houses of the sailors at first sight seem dilapidated but then one discovers interesting evocative corners and vistas in the intricate network of streets in the historical center. Almost suspended on the water, Trapani is white, luminous. The light arrives from the sea, like the scirocco, with white houses, white glittering salt pads scattered in a checkerboard along the coast.

This city has astutely blended its age-old heritage, Greek elegance, Phoenician enterprise and skill, Arab indolence and voluptuousness into something indefinably mysterious. Profoundly Mediterranean, a seafaring port city, today it tends more to fishing and tourism, as point of departure for the islands, and no longer trade and commerce, crossroads of people and merchants as in the past when its role as bridge between Africa and Spain guaranteed it prestige, wealth, and autonomy. The economy, as in the past, depends on tuna fishing, salt, the working

◀ ▲ Spiral staircase of the bell tower and fourteenth-century frescoes in the Church of San Domenico.

of coral from its seas (with techniques learned from Arabs and Jews), and – from the late 18th century – the cultivation of grapes, and the making of excellent wines.

Corso Vittorio Emanuele and *Via Garibaldi* are the principal streets of the narrow historical center, while crowded *Via Fardella* is the long street that crosses the nineteenth-century city and the new city from the slopes of Mount Erice. In a few years it became the street for shopping and meeting place for the youth of Trapani, with pubs and discoteques. Most of the monuments are in the historical center and the labyrinth of criss-crossing lanes and streets branches off from Via Garibaldi and Corso Vittorio Emanuele. Via Garibaldi (the old thirteenth-century Rua Nova) is the street created by the Aragonese James II: lined with the seventeenth-century convents, palaces and patrician dwellings and two churches, **Santa Maria dell'Itria** (1621), with a Baroque facade, and **Santa Maria del Soccorso** or **Badia Nuova** built in the 15th century and renovated in Baroque times. The **Church of San Domenico**

nearby, also a Baroque renovation, still has its splendid fourteenth-century rose window, and some of the frescoes inside, in the Pepoli Chapel, also date to that time. A fourteenth-century *wooden Christ* dominates the altar of the Baroque chapel, while a splendid spiral staircase leads to the top of the bell tower.

After crossing Via della Libertà, **Piazza del Mercato del Pesce** lies on the waterfront. The market, and not only of fish, is held every morning under the porticos, with a mixture of colors, odors and cries. Nearby, on the corner of Via Carosio with its overwhelming fragrance of cream and cinnamon, one can't help but stop at the *pasticceria Colicchia*, a historical place in Trapani, to taste the excellent Sicilian cannoli or the jasmine and water-ices.

The former **Church of Sant'Agostino**, in the piazza of the same name, often hosts concerts. It was heavily bombed

▶ The lively porticoed market square in Trapani.

◀▲ Close-up of the Baroque Church of the Jesuit Convent and wooden statues of the *Group of Mysteries*.

in the last war but the fourteenth-century rose window with its interlacing arches, all decorated in openwork, and the Gothic portal came through unscathed. Opposite the church is the **Fountain of Saturn** (16th century) and, nearby, the **Palazzo Senatorio** or **Cavarretta** with three stories decorated with statues, arches and columns and the **Clock Tower**. The **Church of the Jesuit College** of the 17th century, dedicated to the Immaculate Conception, has a sumptuous Baroque facade. In Corso Vittorio Emanuele, the old Rua Grande, is the **Cathedral of San Lorenzo** with the great green dome that dominates the silhouette of the city. Built in the 14th century it was later enlarged and restored in the 17th-18th century by the architects Bonaventura Certo and Giovanni Biagio Amico. It is Latin cross in plan, with a nave and side aisles and contains a *Crucifixion* attributed to Van Dyck. The **Church of Purgatory** nearby, dating to 1688, has a two-tiered facade and is decorated with statues of the apostles. Inside are the **Groups of the Mysteries**, twenty eight life-size wooden statues, carried in procession on Holy Friday. Continuing along the Corso, after the Bastione Imperiale in the old quarters, comes the seventeenth-century **Church of San Liberale**, dedicated to the patron saint of coral fishers, and the **Ligny Tower** built by the viceroy, Prince Claudio La Moraldo, in 1671 in defense of the city. It now houses the **Museo della Preistoria e del Mare** (Museum of Prehistory and of the Sea) with a collection of objects, photographs, documents that illustrate the prehistory of Trapani.

◀ The lovely green dome of the Cathedral of San Lorenzo, landmark in the skyline, and interior.

◄ ▲ The Ligny Tower, seat of the Museum of Prehistory and of the Sea and one of the rooms.

Retracing our steps, in the Jewish quarter, in the heart of the historical center in Via Giudecca is the Gothic **Palazzo della Giudecca** built in 1439 by the aristocratic Ciambra family.

The **Shrine of the Annunziata** is one of the most important monuments in the city and is held dear by the citizens of Trapani because inside is the *Madunnuzza*. Built by the Carmelites in 1224, the church was later extended. In 1770 it was remodeled in Baroque style by the architect Giovanni Biagio Amico. The actual shrine is behind the high altar, the **Chapel of the Madonna** of 1661, a triumph of polychrome marbles with paintings on the walls by Andrea Marrone depicting Jewish history. Beneath a baldachin supported by eight marble columns is the so-called "*Madonna and Child of Trapani*", a masterpiece of grace and perfection, and the devotion of the cit-

izens to this Madonna thought to be miraculous is still strong with pilgrimages continuously arriving. This statue is one of the rare examples of Tuscan fourteenth-century art in Sicily and seems to have been commissioned from Andrea Pisano by the consul of Pisa.

▼ ► The tower of the old Palazzo della Giudecca in the Jewish quarter and the Shrine of the Annunziata which houses the venerated "Madunnuzza".

▲ ► The Good Friday Procession and the fourteenth-century *Madonna and Child*, known as "*Madunnuzza*", by the school of Pisano.

The **Convent** of the **Church of the Carmelites**, with a monumental staircase known as "magnifico" inside and a Renaissance **Cloister**, is today the headquarters of the **Museo Regionale Pepoli** with an important collection of archaeological material, sculpture, paintings, examples of the goldsmith's art, silver and creations in coral such as crucifixes and above all the splendid *coral lamp*, with enamels and gold, by Fra' Matteo Bavera. A *Saint Francis with the Stigmata*, painted by Titian in 1530, holds forth in the sixth room of the museum.

▲ ► Cloister of the Pepoli Museum, *coral lamp* by Fra' Matteo Bavera and coral *Crucifix*.

ISLAND OF PANTELLERIA

▲▼ The bay of Cala Gadir with the small harbor and the *Arco dell'Elefante*, a natural rock sculpture and symbol of Pantelleria.

The remoteness of wild and impervious Pantelleria, an island in the Strait of Sicily, is both its fortune and an atavistic burden. Only seventy kilometers separate it from Tunisia, a hundred and ten from Sicily.

This black island, the largest of the Sicilian islands, emerged from the blue African sea when a submarine volcano exploded two hundred thousand years ago and signs of its origins are evident in the cone of *Montagna Grande*, 835 meters high. The *favare*, high jets of water vapor emerging from the clefts and crevices of the rock, are as spell-binding as the **Specchio di Venere**, or Venus's mirror, at **Cala Denti**, a lake inside a crater fed by bubbling hot sulphur springs. Pantelleria, an island of rare beauty, will never let you down. This "black pearl of the Mediterranean", halfway between fire and water, has a subtle bewitching charm. The colors of the sea range from azure to emerald green to blue, and the ocean bottom as at **Cala Tramontano** is a true paradise for scuba divers with exotic as well as indigenous fish and banks of red, rose-colored and rare black coral, meadows of *poseidonia oceanica*, red gorgonians and sponges. The jagged coastline conceals innumerable bays, grottoes, rocks and bluffs falling sheer to the sea, as at **Cala Levante** between the *Faraglione* and the *Arco dell'Elefante*, naturally formed sculptures that have become the symbols of Pantelleria, or **Cala Gadir** with its fishing harbor, and hot water spa.

◀ ▼ Venus's mirror, a sulphur lake inside a crater and the romantic hot water Grotto of Sataria.

white flowers, and the terraced vineyards and olive groves that cover the island make the black lava landscape extraordinarily human. The around 8000 Panteschi, as the inhabitants are called, are traditionally farmers rather than sailors. The fauna of Pantelleria consists of colonies of wild rabbits, seagulls and the rare Greek turtles, who come here to lay their eggs, and a host of migratory birds on their way to Africa.

More hospitable sites where one can stretch out on the reefs, the *balate*, are at **Punta Sidere**, **Marina di Suvaki** and **Bue Marino**. The best-known and most photographed however is the **Balata dei Turchi**, one of the wildest and most solitary, with obsidian quarries and cliffs three hundred meters high falling sheer to the sea, where the pirates landed after their raids. The more romantic tourists will love the **Lago delle Ondine** or **Sirene** at *Punta Spillo*, pools of water nestling in volcanic rocks, and **Grotta di Sataria**, is one of the most fascinating corners of the island where Homer has Calypso cast her spell on Ulysses.

The green-cloaked mountains with their oak forests, the maritime and Aleppo pines, the Mediterranean maquis, whortleberries, mulberries, capers with their evanescent

In Pantelleria the Arabs worked a miracle: they transformed the harsh island into a sort of Eden, a fertile garden of citrus trees, mulberries, palms, vineyards and olives, which they planted lower than the other plants and set in enclosures of lava stone to protect them from the wind. Low grapevines abound and the olive trees, heavy with large exquisite olives, have been pruned to keep them low to the ground. These stone gardens are a distinctive feature of Pantelleria, as are the *dammusi*, the Arab houses, square or rectangular and built of dry masonry lava stone with "vaulted roofs". Today the *dammusi* are splendid summer homes for celebrities such as the

► The characteristic dwellings of Pantelleria known as "*dammusi*" and *sese*, a funerary monument of the Sesiote people.

fashion designer Giorgio Armani, or movie stars such as Claudia Cardinale or Gerard Depardieux, as well as journalists, politicians, photographers. Most of them continue growing the zibbibo grapes (from the Arab *zabib*), used to make the *Passito di Pantelleria*.

In Neolithic times, the island was favored by the Sesiote people from the coasts of Africa, similar to the Siculi, who settled in the village of **Mursia**. They came for the obsidian, a black volcanic glass, the "gold" of prehistory and in demand throughout the Mediterranean. They left various traces of their presence in Pantelleria, from the **Cyclopic Wall**, built to defend the village – the most imposing of prehistory – to the **sesi**, large hemispherical funeral monuments, similar to the Sardinian *nuraghi*, with sepulchral cells inside dug out of the stone.

A surfaced road fifty kilometers long runs around the entire island. Beginning at the town of **Pantelleria** – capital of the island with its houses clustered around the **Castello di Barbacane** and the small square that reaches to the sea – delightful white villages line the road, one after the other, with something Near Eastern in their names, the labyrinth of steep lanes and alleys, the square houses, the courtyards full of flowers like the *casbah* of a medina, and in the dialect, a mix-

ture of Arabian-Sicilian-Pantesco. The odors of the cuisine that fill the air bring to mind the Berbers, with fish *couscous*, *sciakisciuka*, vegetable *caponata*, delicate ravioli filled with ricotta and mint, or chicken with capers, and *tuma*, goat cheese seasoned with capers and oil. And most Arabian of all, the *mustazzola*, a real temptation: puff paste filled with a mixture of semolina, mulled wine, cinnamon, candied orange peel and spices, all accompanied by a glass of Passito *doc*. To take home from Pantelleria, besides the wine and capers, are the zibbibo marmelades and jellies.

◄ The capers growing everywhere are a basic ingredient in the cuisine of Pantelleria.

PASSION FOR PASSITO

D ried zibbibo grapes are used to make Passito. This fine sweet suave wine, dense and liqueur-like, is the vaunt of Sicilian and in particular Pantesco enology and is the speciality of the island, esteemed throughout the world.

A golden yellow in color, *Passito di Pantelleria* has a velvety taste, pleasing and typical of zibbibo, with an apricot and peach aroma, and with an alcoholic gradation of 14.5° that goes well with desserts, but also with some cheeses. The local farmers say it is a wine suited to lovers, helps meditation, and is excellent to savor in company.

The zibbibo grape was known to the Egyptians, who ended their meals with a beverage obtained from raisins, three thousand years ago. In Pantelleria the grape was introduced and cultivated by the Phoenicians (who landed on the island they called *Yrnim* – island of wind and seagulls). The Arabs improved its cultivation and the drying of the grapes.

▲ Bottles of Moscato and Passito wine.

The low vines (on Pantelleria they cover 70% of the entire island) are grown in terraces on a black volcanic terrain, and mature in an African sun. The yield is limited and it takes 100 kilos of fresh zibbibo grapes to produce 60 kilos of raisins which in turn give 25/30 liters of wine. The zibbibo grapes are large, white and sweet and are also delicious as table grapes. After the August vintage they are put to dry in the sun on stone racks in the vineyards for ten days. The bunches are turned often, and then pressed.

The sweet must is fermented for over three months, after which the wine is transferred to small oak barrels left partially open so the carbon dioxide can escape. The slow aging process that can last from four to eight years begins a year later, when they are closed. Eventually this sweet liquorous nectar, the gold of Pantelleria, will be bottled and labeled with the D.O.C. mark as *Passito di Pantelleria* and *Moscato Passito di Pantelleria*.

► The low terraced vineyards of zibbibo grapes.

EGADI ISLANDS

▲ The lovely Bay of Cala Rossa at Favignana.

The mini-archipelago of Trapani, with only 4410 inhabitants, mostly fishermen and farmers, consists of the three islands of Marettimo, Levanzo, Favignana, the islet of Formica, Maraone and the shoal of Porcelli that can be reached by ferry or hydrofoil. They are characterized by a hot mild climate, peace and quiet with rocky bays, coves, beaches of white sand washed by a clear sea, and a sea bottom rich in flora and fauna. To safeguard the area the Region of Sicily has instituted a reserve: the "*Area marina protetta delle Egadi*" (523 sq. km.), the largest in Italy.

The Egadi are islands smelling of Mediterranean maquis, capers, liquorice, and salt air, covered by a flourishing vegetation of 500 species of plants, some of them rare, an ideal stopover for a multitude of migratory birds. It is a dream for naturalists, scuba divers, bird watchers, and hikers. The Egadi are known as the tuna islands, and fishing was connected to the ancient rite of the "*mattanza*". The islands were inhabited in prehistoric times, and Homer called them Tera, Forbazia and Egusa. There is an archaeological park on the ocean bottom, a museum that for thousands of years has safeguarded wrecks, bronzes, amphoras, vases, every so often returned by the sea.

MARETTIMO is the island furthest away from Trapani (38 km.) the wildest and most mountainous, and the loveliest of the three. It has few facilities for mass tourism (only three trattorias, two caffes, a small residence, and no hotels) and this is part of its charm. It is a real paradise for an alternative vacation where the spirit is restored in the midst of nature, solitude and the beauty of the sea. It was the ancient *Hiera*, the island sacred to the Greeks. Basically Marettimo is nothing but a piazza, a church, a few square white fishermen's houses, with terraced Arab rooftops, the windows painted blue or green, and with fuchsia or red bougainvilleas climbing up the walls all along the bay, facing the small fishing port.

▼ ► Sacred aedicule and the peninsula of Punta Troia with the Arab Castle at Marettimo.

◀ ▲ Capers growing between the rocks of Cala Rossa at Favignana and the town of Levanzo with its small harbor.

the village, in **Case Romane**, are the ruins of a Roman house and a small temple of the first century A.D.

LEVANZO is the smallest of the Egadi Islands and the closest to the coast of Trapani, rocky and arid in certain zones. Pasture for the ever-present goats and sheep, with vineyards, rows of prickly pears and agaves, gulls and other birds nesting, such as the eagle. Vacations here mean passion and love for the sea and nature, a rediscovery of the dimension of time and silence, regeneration of the body and the soul. **Cala Tramontano** and **Cala Minnola** (that in dialect means almond) are charming small beaches, with rocks rising sheer from the sea, and an ocean bed rich in Carthaginian and Roman archaeological finds, fish of all kinds and colors, including the pearl shell, which arrived here from the Indian Ocean after the opening of the Suez Canal. **Punta Pesce** is another beach, guarded by two massive *faraglioni*, where one can swim in absolute calm. There are two hotels in Levanzo, two restaurants and one bar, a single road that crosses the entire and sole village of white houses.

Levanzo is known for its grottos. The best known is the **Grotta dei Genovesi** that overlooks the sea, with pre-

To visit are the **Grotta del Cammello**, sheltering a small pebbly beach and a turquoise sea for bathing, and the **Grotta del Presepio**, or nativity scene, so-called because of the shapes of the rocks, eroded by wind and water. The sound of the waves echoes strongly in the **Grotta della Bombarda**. On the cliff of the small peninsula of Punta Troia is a fortress-like **Castle** built by the Arabs. Above

historic graffiti and Neolithic rock paintings, symbols of a civilization of ten thousand years ago discovered by chance in 1949 by an enterprising teacher. The graffiti and paintings depicting scenes of the hunt, animals, deer, tuna fish and human beings are quite elegant. It is accessible on foot in about two hours.

FAVIGNANA is a butterfly-shaped island on the blue African sea. The name is derived from the *Favonio*, the prevailing wind. For Homer it was *Aegades*, the Island of Goats where the wandering Ulysses landed before returning to Ithaca. It is the principal town of the Egadi Islands, the largest in the archipelago, and is considered the "queen" where thousands of tourists land each year.

The wild nature is redolent of capers, oregano and black basil. The sea is extraordinary with its clear water and its seabed rich in coral (also black coral) and with an exceptional variety of fish including exotic species from the Red Sea. The bays and the beaches of **Cala Burrone** and **Cala Rotonda** are lovely, and the bay of **Cala Azzurra** has two tiny beaches of fine white sand, as in the tropics. The most fascinating, with its emerald sea, is the bay of **Cala Rossa**, a name that calls up ancient memories of war. It was in this amphitheater-shaped bay sloping down to

the sea that the Romans hid with their ships, led by Lutatius Catulus, prior to a surprise attack on Hanno's Carthaginian fleet. Right in front of Cala Rossa is another evocative setting, that of the **Cave di Tufo**, or tufa quarries. These enormous masses of quaternary stone with tall walls and marked by hundreds of horizontal cuts were used for building material back in antiquity, since tufa was easy to cut and work. But Favignana calls to mind the tuna fish, the *tonnara*, the *mattanza*. Every year between 1500 and 2000 tons of tuna fish are processed, and this island holds the record for canned tuna, first packaged by the **Tonnara Florio**, dominating the harbor, and owned by the Florio family.

Another attraction of Favignana is the **Bagno delle Donne**, or women's bath, in the zone of San Nicola, an enormous pool of sea water excavated in the rock where one can still go swimming. It is known as *murenario*, because this is where the Romans raised the moray eels for one of their favorite dishes. The pool still communicates with the sea by way of a subterranean conduit.

▼ The small pink beach and the town of Favignana.

THE SONG OF THE RÀIS

I t takes a hundred days to prepare the *mattanza*, the final act in the complex ritual for hunting and killing the tuna, a bloody rite, unforgettable and spectacular, charged with religious and cultural symbolism.

Shoals of tuna fish arrive from the ocean to reproduce in the warm limpid waters of Sicily from April to June. This is when the *tonnaroti* lay a complicated system of nets, the *tonnare* anchored to floats, in the sea: The tuna enter and are forced to move from one enclosure to another through gates. A few days before the *mattanza*, the *camera della morte* or death chamber is prepared.

On the day established by the *ràis* (the chief of *mattanza*) the *tonnaroti* position their boats, known as *muciare*, on three sides of a rectangle. The *ràis* coordinates the entire operation and puts his boat at the center of the chamber into which all the tuna fish have been rounded up. As the *tonnaroti* draw in the heavy nets, their heaving and hauling is accompanied by propitiatory songs and invocations to Jesus and the saints, the *cialome*. The thrashing tuna fish are speared or hooked one by one and killed, and hauled onto the flatboat that closes the fourth side of the rectangle while the water turns red.

The success of the *mattanza* is entrusted to the *ràis, lu raisi,* the chief, including the preparation that begins a hundred days earlier, when by him-

▲▼ Tuna fish counter at the fish market and *mattanza*, the tuna kill.

◄ ▲ Florio: the "queen of tuna fisheries" and the fish market at Favignana.

self he sounds the sea bottom to identify the places where the nets are to be cast to make it easier for the tuna to pass. The *ràis* commands, and his orders are indisputable. If the catch is poor, his career is over. The following year someone else will take his place.

These methods go back to ancient times and led to the founding of cities, hamlets and towns. Fishing and trade provided work, fed and created wealth for entire generations.

There were once more than 50 *tonnare* or tuna fisheries in Sicily. The one in Scopello dates to the 13th century and belonged to Frederick II of Swabia (the restored premises are rented out for vacations). Most of the *tonnare* have closed. A few reserve the spectacle for the growing number of tourists.

They survive in Favignana, San Giuliano and Capo Passero. Projects for a cultural and study center in the fifty hectares of the **Florio tuna fisheries** of Favignana, a gem of industrial architecture which produced the first tin of canned tuna, are under way. Not a single part of the tuna, considered the "pig of the sea", goes to waste. Processing pays off: the *lattume* are sold fresh to be fried, or conserved in brine, or dried in the sun. The *bottarga* or roe is dried in the sun, or preserved in oil or salt as are the stomach, the intestines, the heart, and the lungs. The *tonnina*, the sushi of the Japanese, that is the belly and the *busonaglia* are preserved in salt in wooden barrels while the head, the tail and the spine are boiled to extract an oil widely used in industry.

▼ The tuna fishery of Piano Battaglia at Scopello, where the *mattanza* still takes place.

ISLE OF MOZIA

Mozia, ancient *Motya*, a tiny flat low island, is one of the most charming and seductive places in Sicily with a landscape of lagoons, a checkerboard of saltpans and windmills. There are only nine inhabitants. But there is a museum, and expanses of ancient ruins, migratory birds, olive trees, Aleppo pines, agaves, Mediterranean maquis, and vineyards that reach to the sea. Silence and an ancient history are enclosed in the forty hectares of the island.

Together with the Longa, Santa Maria and Scuola islands, Mozia forms the small *Arcipelago dello Stagnone*: a Natural Lagoon Reserve where the sea is barely a meter deep. The island is easy to reach by motorboat in a few minutes crossing a small arm of water but it is most fun to walk out on the causeway during low tide.

Mozia is a Phoenician stretch of land. It was founded in the 8th century B.C. by the small Semite populace that came from the Near East and settled in western Sicily.

▼ ► The cothon, Punic careenage basin, the only one in Sicily and the stele of the Punic goddess Tanit.

Motya means spinnery and the city was full of shops and warehouses for the weaving and dying of textiles with vermilion (a substance that was derived from a mollusk, the murex) and that they then sold to the peoples of the Mediterranean. The Phoenician name too is derived from the Greek *phoinix* which means red-purple.

Mozia became an opulent and prosperous colony with its own coinage, welcoming foreigners, and roads and bridges were built, and even a **cothon** (a careenage basin), the only one in Sicily and just like one found in Carthage. The Phoenicians, skilful and enterprising navigators and merchants, competed with the Greeks of Sicily for the supremacy of the Mediterranean but also traded with them. Motya was in a strategic geographic position.

◀ Terracotta statuette in the Whitaker Museum.

sius. The few survivors abandoned the island and withdrew to the coast where they founded a new city, *Lilybaeum*, now Marsala. Motya fell into oblivion and was never rebuilt, not even by the Carthaginians when they took it back. It was a wealthy English nobleman with a passion for archaeology, Joseph Whitaker, who rediscovered Mozia. He bought the island, at the time called San Pantaleo, in the early twentieth century and began an excavation campaign which brought to light quantities of fine masterpieces: ceramics, vases, amphoras, sculpture, jewellery, and statuettes of the Great Mother.

Thus in 397 B.C. the tyrant Dionysius of Syracuse finally succeeded in wiping out Motya, for the Carthaginian fleet which came to its defense could do nothing against the seven hundred ships and ten thousand soldiers of Diony-

Ten thousand objects and finds are now in the **Whitaker Museum**. In one of the last excavations of 1979, the

▼ The old North Gate of Mozia.

◀ The elegant and sensuous *Ephebus of Motya*,
symbol of the meeting of Punic and Greek cultures.

extraordinarily elegant marble statue of the **Ephebus of Motya** (now in the museum) was found, without arms or feet, a hundred and eighty centimeters tall and unlike the classic nude figures, he wears a long clinging pleated garment that accentuates his sensuous forms. Historians are still not certain as to his identity, perhaps a magistrate or a priest, certainly a noble, judging from his haircut and the tight band around his chest.

The ephebus is in any case the symbol of that extraordinary and special encounter-clash in ancient Sicily of Greek and Phoenician-Punic civilization of which we are all the offspring and the heir.

The excavations uncovered two houses: the **House of the Amphoras** with only one room where a large quantity of Phoenician amphoras were found and the **House of the Mosaics**, of Greek origin, built in 397 B.C. on Phoenician foundations, elegant with a peristyle and a pavement decorated with mosaics. Near the house are a small **Barracks**, a military building, and the remains of the **South Gate** of the 5th century B.C., one of the four gates leading into the city. The **Archaic Necropolis**, the oldest in Mozia, stretches out on the shores of the sea and along the walls. But the most interesting area is the **Tophet** or sacred area next to the necropolis, a Semite sanctuary and place of worship where children were sacrificed. Inside, in a triangular area, are the remains of a small temple into which only the priest could enter. Historians today say that only stillborn children were sacrificed. Between the **North Gate** and the Necropolis are the ruins of another 5th century B.C. sanctuary, known as **Cappiddazzu**, dedicated to Astarte, the goddess of beauty and fertility.

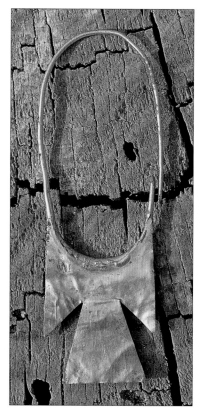

▶ Punic ornament
in the Whitaker Museum.

▲▼ The Tophet, sacred sanctuary where children were sacrificed and the mosaic floor of the elegant House of the Mosaics.

MARSALA

T he world Marsala brings to mind something sweet, fragrant, delicious: the famous wine. An amber-colored nectar, the inseparable companion of cakes, ice cream, desserts and zabaglione, sprinkled with... marsala. The history and fortunes of this wine are connected to an English merchant from Liverpool, a connoisseur of fortified wines. He improved the wine and it landed on the tables of English gourmets: this was the beginning of the Sicilian wine-making industry.

▲▼ Vineyards for the production of the sweet Marsala wine and the seafront with palms of the saltpans of Marsala.

Marsala is a provincial city full of fascinating secrets, something like its wine. Vivacious and with its share of monuments, art and lovely beaches but with a more reticent style of architecture. Well-kept and full of flourishing gardens, culturally alive and open to innovations, it is in a sense the international drawing room of this part of Sicily. It lives on agriculture, wine making and tourism, the latter increasingly important with the English coming in ever greater numbers although this has been their domicile of choice for three centuries. Marsala has ten kilometers of white beaches, a crystal clear blue sea which has been awarded the "blue flag" for clean waters for the last ten year. Two events in Marsala every year are fully booked: wine and jazz are the undisputed protagonists of an exceptional sodality in the *Marsala Doc Festival*, an international review of jazz artists and concerts held every year in July. The other event, part religious, part folklore, is the *Procession of the Passion of Christ* on the eve of Good Friday in which the citizens take part dressed as saints.

Marsala is the ancient *Lilybaeum*, a name given by the Phoenicians who fortified it so strongly that in 368 B.C. it was able to hold out against Dionysius the Younger, the tyrant of Syracuse. The Romans succeeded in occupying it and built opulent villas and roads. In 204 B.C. Scipio Africanus left from the harbor of Marsala to invade Carthage. Decadence and oblivion however eventually arrived. It was not till 830 that the Arabs revived the city and its historical port and their traces are still visible. Marsala remained an important trading center under the Normans who brought in Christianity and built numerous churches. The city suddenly found itself in the limelight again on May 11, 1860 when Garibaldi with his Thousand chose it as the place to land in Sicily in his efforts to drive the Bourbons from the island and reunite Italy under a single banner. May 11 was once more a fateful day in 1943 when half the city was razed to the ground by allied bombings.

Only three *insulae* or city blocks remain of the Roman *Lilybaeum*, with the remains of luxurias **Villas**, and a particularly fine bath building from the 3rd century B.C. with a polychrome mosaic floor and geometric decorations, as well as others with animals. The pillars that permitted the passage of hot air are intact.

Near the sea, next to the important archaeological site and the **Museum**, is the small **Church of San Giovanni**, with a splendid Baroque portal, built over a grotto, the cave of the legendary *Sibyl of Lilybaeum*. Both the church and the grotto are pilgrim sites, and the faithful pray and bathe in the water during the *feast of Saint John*.

The two monumental city gates of Marsala, **Porta Nuova** and **Porta Garibaldi**, lead to the city and the historical center. *Piazza della Repubblica* is the pedestrian parlor

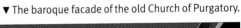
▼ The baroque facade of the old Church of Purgatory.

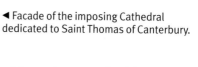

◄ Facade of the imposing Cathedral dedicated to Saint Thomas of Canterbury.

with two imposing buildings, **Palazzo Senatoriale** and the **Cathedral**. The Cathedral, begun in Norman times, was not finished until the early twentieth century and was then bombed during World War II. Dedicated to Saint Thomas of Canterbury, columns separate the nave from the side aisles. Adjacent premises house the **Tapestry Museum** with eight precious sixteenth-century Flemish tapestries depicting the *War waged by emperor Titus against the Jews*.

Leading off the piazza is *Via XI Maggio*, known as the "Càssaro", with shops and boutiques. Lanes, Arab alleys, and flowering patios branch off from the street. The **Monastery of San Pietro** of the Benedictine sisters, a sixteenth-century monumental complex now restored, is also here. At the corner of the monastery is a square tower with two tiers of loggias, known as the **Specola**. The monastery is now a cultural center housing a Library and the **Garibaldi Museum**. In *Piazza del Carmine*, with patrician palaces, some of them Baroque, is the **Convent of the Carmine** of 1155. The convent has been well restored and houses the **Museum of Contemporary Art**.

◄ ▼ Flemish tapestry in the Tapestry Museum and the monumental 16th century Monastery of San Pietro.

A DOC MARSALA

During prohibition the United States outlawed all alcohol, but not Marsala which despite its 18 degrees could be freely sold because it was considered medicinal. This historic Anglo-Sicilian wine was the first to have the *Doc* mark (*denominazione di origine controllata*, or State designated label of controlled quality) and one of the four wines in the world recognized as a dessert wine. It owes its fortunes to John Woodhouse, an English merchant, a connoisseur, who improved it and sent it to the tables of his English friends. So that it would keep during the long trip from Sicily, he added alcohol, and this was marsala.

It was 1773, and the wine-making industry got its start. Others followed him in this venture, Ingham, another Englishman who had come to Sicily to buy soda, and in 1831 Vincenzo Florio from Calabria, Sicilian by adoption.

Marsala wine is now sold in thirty-five countries, while the production zone is the territory between Marsala and Trapani, around eighty-seven thousand hectares which yield eight million liters of wine a year, produced and bottled by twenty firms, some of which can be visited by appointment.

To truly appreciate this fragrant liqueur wine it must be cool, at a temperature of 12-14° C, possibly in small tall-footed tulip shaped glasses. As a sweet wine it is a dessert wine; dry or semi-dry, it is ideal for accompanying cheeses. The color, from gold to amber to ruby, is the result of aging. Marsala can be *Fine* – aged for more than a year, *Superior* – aged for over two years, while the *Superiore Riserva* requires four years of aging and the *Vergine Solares Riserva*, ten years.

The sugar content of the white grapes, varieties called Grillo, Catarratto, Inzolia, and Damaschino, is high, while Pignatello, Calabrese and Nerello Mascalese grapes are used for the ruby red Marsala. The Grillo grapevines are autochthonous and have been grown in Sicily since 300 B.C., brought there by the Greeks. The fruity aroma ranges from apricot, date, plum for the Superiore Riserva; raisin and vanilla for the Marsala Superiore, but always with a velvety aftertaste.

▲▼ Early twentieth-century Florio poster and the Florio wine cellars.

MAZARA DEL VALLO

◄ ▲ Lanes and alleys in the *casbah* in the historical center.

Mazara, one of the most important deep-sea fishing towns in Italy, is in the farthest point of Sicily, in "the Italian Africa".

The heart of Mazara is its old historical center, where the Islamic heritage comes to the fore in the labyrinth of courtyards, flowering gardens, small squares, lanes and blind alleys, as much of a tangle as the *casbah* in an Arab *medina*, and that is just what the people of Mazara call it. Shops, houses, colors, odors, and music, Arab music, arrives from every window and fills the streets. The men wear white caftans and the typical headdress, the women are almost all veiled. Even the language, a mixture of Arab and Sicilian, makes one think one is in the Maghreb. This is Mazara del Vallo, from the Phoenician name meaning "castle". The square-shaped city stretches out along both shores of the Mazaro River, bearing witness to its ancient past. There is a tree-shaded waterfront with palms and magnolias and bars and restaurants offering traditional and Arab cuisine based on fish.

Mazara's history begins with the Phoenicians who landed here and set up their trading posts. It then became a colony and port of powerful Selinunte. On June 17, 827, the Arabs put ashore at Mazara, from Capo Granitola, to occupy Byzantine Sicily. After seventy-five years of war the island, where they remained for almost two centuries, was

▼ Overlooking the roofs of the city.

▲ ▼ Couscous, a typical dish of Mazara, and the balcony of a fisherman's house.

▲ The busy canal port of Mazara del Vallo.

theirs. The city was enriched with monuments and the economy and population grew. The Arabs used innovative techniques in fishing and agriculture, introducing the cultivation of oranges, mulberries, cotton and sugar cane, in addition to the wheat. In 1072 Great Count Roger's Normans defeated the Saracens of Emir Mokarta and brought in Christianity, built churches, convents and monasteries and instituted the first parliament in the world. In 1820 the city participated in the revolutionary uprisings. Later, like all of Sicily, it supported Garibaldi and his army.

Via Bagno is the main street in the *casbah*, in Mazara's historical center, the old Saracen quarter. The **Church of Santa Veneranda** (Piazza Santa Veneranda) is located in

◄ ▼ The Church of Santa Veneranda with a wrought-iron balcony and the apses of the Church of San Nicolò Regale.

▲ ▶ Bas-relief on the portal of the Cathedral with *Roger on horseback trampling a Muslim* and the lavish nave.

the labyrinth of alleyways and lanes. It was restored in the 17th-18th century with a wrought iron balcony and a lavish Baroque facade with twin bell towers. Nearby are the **Convent** and **Church of San Michele** built in the 11th century by George of Antioch, and then renovated in the 17th century. The Norman **Church of San Nicolò Regale** overlooking the harbor was built in stone in 1124 with a square plan and three apses surmounted by a dome.

Piazza della Repubblica, the Baroque drawing room of Mazara (formerly Piano Maggiore) is the focal point of the city, completely rebuilt in the 17th-18th century. The neoclassic portico of the **Seminario dei Chierici** is the most lavish building on the square. Facing it is the **Bishop's Palace**, built around 1596. The most imposing monument in this fine piazza is the **Cathedral**. Built in 1093 by the Normans on the ruins of the Great Mosque, it was frequently rebuilt. There is a sixteenth-century bas-relief on the portal, depicting *Count Roger on horseback trampling a Muslim*. The interior of the Cathedral is striking with a profusion of gold stuccoes, frescoes and statues. Columns separate the nave from the side aisles and it has three apses.

▶ The splendid *Dancing Satyr* of the 4th century B.C.

One of the finest works is the sixteenth-century *Transfiguration*, a marble group of seven statues by the Sicilian sculptors Antonello and Antonio Gagini. A bas-relief of 1525 by Bartolomeo Berrettaro, in the right aisle, decorates a door that leads to the Cathedral **Museum**, while there is a polychrome marble *Christ* in the left transept.

The former **Jesuit College** now hosts the **Municipal Museum** which contains paintings, archaeological finds, medieval sculpture in Arab style. In the nearby Piazza Plebiscito are the **Churches of the Carmine** and **of Sant'Egidio**. The latter contains the **Archaeological Museum** with the famous *Dancing Satyr*, a splendid Greek bronze dating to the 4th century B.C. that was found in 1998 by fishermen of Mazara del Vallo on the bottom of the Strait of Sicily. The statue shows a leaping satyr, his left leg raised and his head thrown back.

SELINUNTE

Thirty kilometers of fertile countryside with olives, grapes, wheat and agaves separate Mazara del Vallo from Selinunte, and the sea that washes the sandy beach of Marinella. The city of Selinunte, once the westernmost of the Greek colonies, is now a pile of ancient ruins and stones, some set upright, silhouetted against the sea in a solemn magical landscape. In the 6th and 5th centuries B.C. nine temples were built, imposing and magnificent, decorated with statues and metopes, the finest examples of Doric architecture. Not much remains, yet no other place (two hundred and fifty hectares, one of the largest archaeological parks in Europe) gives one the feeling of the relentless onward march of time, the brutality of history, the violence of nature in its earthquakes.

▲▼ One of the metopes from the Temples of Selinunte (Archaeological Museum of Palermo) and view of Temples C and D.

▲ Temple E still has part of its trabeation.

For the Greeks Selinunte was *Selinon*, the name of the sweet-smelling parsley that still grows wild in the area, and of the river *Selinon*, now Modione, at the mouth of which the Greeks founded the city in the 7th century B.C. Beautiful, rich and powerful Selinunte, described by Virgil as full of palms, was the only Greek city allied to Carthage in the Sicilian Punic war which ended in 480 B.C. with the defeat of the Carthaginians at Himera. Selinunte then allied itself to Syracuse and in 409 B.C., at the height of its splendor, the Carthaginian Hannibal pulled down the walls and sacked the temples. In 250 B.C. in order to prevent the city from falling into Roman hands, the Carthaginians destroyed most of it and a violent earthquake in the Middle Ages did away with whatever remained of the once glorious Selinunte.

Selinunte was rediscovered in the 16th century by the Dominican historian Tommaso Fazello but excavation did not begin until the nineteenth century with the English. A bronze statue known as the *Ephebus of Selinunte* came from the excavations. It is now in the Museum of Castelvetrano. The nude ephebus is 85 centimeters tall, with beautiful vigorous forms, a masterpiece of Greek art, one of the finest works of art in Italy according to the art historian Cesare Brandi. The archaeological park is divided into four zones: the Acropolis, the eastern hill, the old city and the sanctuary of Malophoros.

The **Acropolis**, the heart of life of the inhabitants of Selinunte, is on a height dropping sheer to the sea between the Modione (Selinon) and Cottone rivers. And this is where the ruins of the oldest temples are. Very little remains of **Temples O** and **A**, close together and very alike, dating to the 5th century B.C.; nor is much left of the small Hellenistic **Temple B**, probably dedicated to the Agrigento philosopher Empedocles.

◀ The vigorous 5th century B.C.
Ephebus of Selinunte (Museum of Castelvetrano)

▲ A haunting picture of Temple C and a Punic mosaic in the foreground.

▲◄ The ruins of the Sanctuary of Malòphoros.

cent **Temple E**, dating to the 5th century B.C., with its harmonious proportions dominates the immense and evocative landscape of ruins. In perfect Doric style, it is a hexastyle peripteral temple with thirty-eight columns and was partially reconstructed in the 1960s.

Temple F, the smallest and most poorly preserved, dates to 550-540 B.C. and is more archaic in style. **Temple G** is the largest in Selinunte, covering an area of 6120 square meters. Dedicated to the god Apollo it was 30 meters high and stood in a spectacular position. Today it is nothing but ruins. One column has been raised at the center making it all the more melancholy and tragic. It seems not to have been finished when the earthquake destroyed the city in 409 B.C. Not far from the Acropolis are the ruins of the **Sanctuary of the Malòphoros** ("she who bears the pomegranate"), perhaps consecrated to Demeter Malòphoros, the goddess of plants and fertility since terracotta statuettes of female divinities holding a pomegranate have

The 6th century B.C. **Temple C**, perhaps the oldest and largest on the Acropolis (64 by 24 meters), is hexastyle peripteral, in other words a porticoed temple with forty-two columns. Fourteen on the north side have been raised. Possibly dedicated to Heracles, the lovely metopes now in the Archaeological Museum in Palermo come from this Temple. Only a few ruins and stones half covered by weeds are all that remain of the 6th century B.C. **Temple D**. Three other temples, **E, F, G**, on the eastern hill, are in much better condition. The imposing and magnifi-

been found in great number. The sanctuary was 60 meters long and 50 wide, with a small *megaron* shaped temple without columns surrounded by a *temenos*, or sacred precinct. In building the temples to their gods the citizens of Selinunte used stone from the neighboring Quarry or *Cave* di **Rocca di Cusa**, a site six kilometers away. Blocks of columns, some cut into drums, and others barely indicated, lie scattered around with weeds growing in the cracks. After twenty-five centuries everything looks as if it were just waiting for work to be resumed. The quarry was however closed in 409 B.C.

All that is left of **HERACLEA MINOA**, the ancient colony of Selinunte, is the splendid **Theater** on the hill of Capo Bianco overlooking the sea.

▼ ► The white Theater of Heraclea Minoa overlooks the sea from the hill of Capo Bianco and blocks of stone from the quarries of Cusa, used by the citizens of Selinunte in building the temple.

AGRIGENTO

Agrigento stands up high on the top of the Girgenti Hills and the Rupe Atenea. Like a sphinx it overlooks the famous age-old Valley of the Temples and the sea. The new city, modern Agrigento, rose against the surviving walls. It is rich in gardens and plants, and is where young people hang out and where the citizens come evenings for a stroll and to admire the illuminated Temples. Agrigento, defined by Pindar as "the loveliest of those where mortals lived" no longer has the glory and wealth of antiquity, that opulence that made Empedocles, the Agrigento philosopher say that his fellow citizens lived in the most unbridled luxury as if they were to die the day after, but that they built as if they were destined for eternity. Despite the unauthorized buildings to be seen everywhere, the city still succeeds in casting its spell on the tourist. Agrigento is proud of its Valley, the custodian of the creations of the Greek genius, and cannot conceal a tinge of sadness at the haste with which most tourists visit its medieval hamlet and its splendid buildings. The sun in Agrigento is African, as is the sky

▲▼ A stepped street in Agrigento and flowering almond trees; panorama of the city from the Valley of Temples.

and the air, with the sticky scirocco blowing in, and the blue sea. The city, its monuments, and the countryside are the yellow ocher color of the tufa. This Agrigento that now seems to be so static and isolated due to the injustice and abuses it has been subjected to, was the mother of the great Hellenic civilization. Empedocles, Pirandello and Sciascia were born here. Tourism has not succeeded

◄ The solitary pine tree and the limestone boulder containing the ashes of Pirandello and the statue of Leonardo Sciascia in Racalmuto.

in transforming habits and life, and it is still marked by the festivals such as the one dedicated to Saint Calogero, who saved the city from the plague. Agrigento has also dedicated a festival to the flowering almond tree: the *sagra del mandorlo in fiore*, a folklore festival held from February 2 to 11 among the temples when the ruins are enveloped in clouds of white flowers, heralding spring. The white sandy beaches are also lovely, like **San Leone**, six kilometers from the city. The white bluffs of the **Scala dei Turchi** (those most photographed) characterize a stretch of coast.

Agrigento is the birthplace of Nobel Prize winner Luigi Pirandello, one of the greatest twentieth-century writers and considered the father of modern Italian and European theater. His plays and novels narrate the privations, the absurdity of the human condition, and the conflict between appearance and truth. Among his plays "Sei personaggi in cerca d'autore" (Six characters in search of an author), "Enrico IV" (Henry IV), and his novels, "Uno, nessuno e centomila". The house where he was born, now a **Museum** containing mementos of the writer, is two kilometers from the city, in the **CAOS** contrada, in the midst of age-old Saracen olive trees.

Leonardo Sciascia, an important writer of the latter part of the twentieth century, was born in the sulphur-rich **RACALMUTO** (*Rahalmut* in Arabic) a town of Arab origins, near Agrigento, where he is also buried in the small cemetery. With extreme lu-

cidity he denounced the atrocities of the mafia, the hopes and dramas of the Sicilians in "Il giorno della civetta" (the Day of the Owl) and "Gli zii di Sicilia" (Sicilian Uncles). A particularly successful author of today is Andrea Camilleri, who set the adventures of his Commissario Montalbano, halfway between a detective and a judicial story, in the landscape, cuisine and world of Sicily.

Akragas is the old name of Agrigento. This is what the colonists of Gela and Rhodes called it after founding Gela and Selinunte so it would be easier to control the Mediterranean and the coasts of Africa. Under the tyrant Theron (488-427 B.C.) the city expanded its territory and flourished. In 406 B.C., after various sieges, the Carthaginians conquered *Akragas* and

► The famous bluffs of the Scala dei Turchi at Realmonte.

destroyed it. Reconquered and rebuilt in the 3rd century B.C. by the Corinthian Timoleon, tyrant of Syracuse, *Akragas* once more flourished. The Romans occupied it in 210 B.C. and named it *Agrigentum*. They revolutionized agriculture and turned the city into a trading center. Next came the Byzantines and the city began to decline. In the 11th century it was conquered by the Arabs who built the new town higher up and abandoned the valley of the gods. Under the Saracens it became the second city on the island after Palermo and was the center of a *Signoria*. The Islamic occupants were replaced in 1087, after a long siege, by the Normans who embellished it with churches and religious buildings.

Before going to the famous Valley a few other monuments of Agrigento should be visited. **Porta di Ponte** leads to the historical center, the elegant main street, Via Atenea, full of shops and patrician residences such as **Palazzo Celano** where Goethe sojourned on his Grand Tour. *Via Atenea* is cut through by lanes and alleys, and flights of stairs. The staircase of the Spirito Santo leads up to the

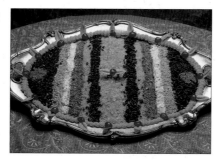

◀ ▼ Sweet couscous, a specialty of the nuns, and the two mullioned windows of the Monastery of Santo Spirito.

abbey of the same name. The **Monastery** and **Church of the Santo Spirito** is a monumental complex founded in the 13th century. It is inhabited by the cloistered Benedictine nuns (only thirteen today) who among the many things they do after their prayers is prepare sublime sweets that can be bought knocking on the convent door. The facade of the convent **church** was frequently restored but still has a fine Gothic portal and a rose window. Of particular note is the **Cloister** of the former medieval monastery, with a fourteenth-century fountain at the center, and the **Chapter Hall** with its splendid entranceway. On the upper floor of the monastery – now municipal property – is an **Anthropological Museum**.

At the end of Via Fodera in Piazzetta del Purgatorio is the Baroque **Church of San Lorenzo** or **of Purgatory**,

◀ ▲ The apses of the Church of Santa Maria de' Greci and Byzantine frescoes inside.

one of the most important in the city and now a **Museum**.

The steep *Via Bac Bac* and *Via Saponara* lead to the small sober **Church of Santa Maria de' Greci** built on the ruins of a 5th century B.C. Doric temple that is visible beneath the left aisle and in the fine flowering courtyard. The church belonged to the Greek clergy and still has its inlaid thirteenth-century portal. The interior with three aisles and three apses has faded Byzantine frescoes.

The **Cathedral** is the tallest building in Agrigento, founded in the eleventh century by Bishop Gerlando, and is flanked by a fifteenth-century bell tower. Ogee arches separate the aisles from the nave in the Latin-cross interior. Figures of *saints* and *nobles* are painted on the sixteenth-century truss ceiling. In the niche in the right aisle is an embalmed body in medieval armor – it is said

to be the mortal remains of San Felice Martire – but for many locals it is that of Brandimarte, the Christian knight in Ariosto's saga, killed by the Saracens at Lampedusa but buried here as Orlando wished. The Cathedral is famous for the curious acoustical phenomenon. If someone speaks, even in a whisper, at the entrance to the church, he can be heard in the apse, eighty-five meters away. In the chapel to the right is the *Urn of Saint Jerome*, an elegant seventeenth-century reliquary in silver. There is a painting of the *Madonna and Child*, attributed to Guido Reni in the **Sacristy**. The Cathedral **Archive** contains the famous *Letter of the devil*, and incomprehensible and obscure epistle written in the seventeenth century, it is said, to Sister Maria Crocifissa Tomasi in the convent of Palma di Montechiaro to lead her into temptation.

▼ ▶ The Arabian Via Bac Bac and the imposing Cathedral of Agrigento dominating the city.

VALLEY OF THE TEMPLES (Valle dei Templi)

The extraordinary moments in which these temples are most evocative are at sunset when they take on an amber hue, and at night when they are illuminated. They are the essence, the summa of art, so close, one behind the other, and overlooking the sea, in a magical unique setting.

Majestic symbols of Greek religion, the temples are surrounded by twisted age-old olive trees and almond trees that envelop them in white blossoms when in flower. Built in barely a century, in the fifth century B.C., in Doric style and in a yellow ocher sandstone tufa, they are the tangible signs of the grandeur of the Greco-Siciliote civilization. The Valley of the Temples, declared a World Heritage Site by UNESCO, covers an area of one thousand two hundred hectares, two kilometers from Agrigento. A panoramic road leads to the archaeological site.

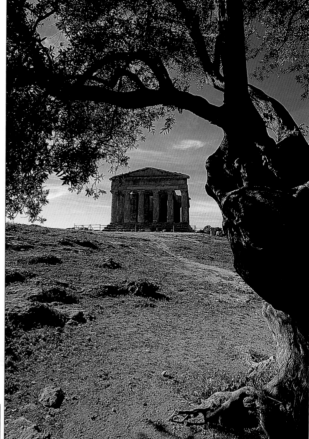

▼ ► The Temple of Hera Lacinia and the Temple of Concord.

▲ The Temple of Hera Lacinia.

The visit begins in the eastern zone, on the highest part of the city, where the **Temple of Hera Lacinia** (Juno, Zeus's wife) stands all by itself. It originally had 34 fluted columns, seven meters high. Only 25 are still standing. Inside there was the *pronaos*, the *cella* with the statue of the goddess at the center, and the *opistòmo* (the back room). The reddish spots on some of the stones in the cella are traces of the fire set by the Carthaginians in 406 B.C. It was restored by the Romans but all ended with the earthquake in the Middle Ages.

The **Temple of Concord**, solemn and imposing, elegant with its geometric Doric lines, simple and perfect in its structure, is still intact after two thousand five hundred years, to bear witness to the greatness of the Greek genius. Built between 430 and 420 B.C., like the others it is in yellow sandstone tufa. It is a hexastyle peripteral temple, 6 fluted columns at the ends and 11 along the sides, 6.75 meters high resting on a stepped stylobate. It was originally faced in polychrome stucco. The entrance to the temple is on the east, as usual, where the sun rises, for the Greeks symbol of life. The monument is still standing because it was transformed into a Byzantine basilica in A.D. 597 and remained such until 1748 when it was restored to its original form. It was

▼ ▶ The solemn imposing Doric Temple of Concord, as seen in a nineteenth-century water color and as it is today.

probably dedicated to Castor and Pollux, but in the 16th century was called "of Concord" because of a Latin inscription that came to light during restoration.

Continuing along the Via Sacra, before the temple of Heracles is the **Palaeo-Christian Necropolis** in the hypogeums of Villa Aurea, known as the "Catacombs of Fragapane".

The **Temple of Heracles (Hercules)**, the oldest and largest of all, dates to the 6th century B.C. It was consecrated to Hercules to whom the citizens of Agrigento dedicated the Herculean festivals. It was destroyed by an earthquake and in 1924 eight of its 38 columns were put back in place.

Before visiting the other archaeological zone, on the west, one can rest and enjoy a refreshing pistachio or lemon granita, or coffee dusted with cocoa, seated at the bar right in front of the columns of the temple of Heracles. Moving down towards the sea, almost facing the temple of Jove (Jupiter) is the **Tomb of Theron**, a massive square monument, with a tower with four Ionic columns and Doric capitals supporting the trabeation. It is actually a monument built by the Romans in the first century A.D. in memory of the thirty thousand who died in conquering Agrigento.

Only a few scattered ruins remain of the **Temple of Zeus (Jupiter)**, erected for the king of the gods in the 5th century B.C. to celebrate the victory of Agrigento over Carthage. It was enormous for the time: with an area of 6,500 sq. m., a length of 112 meters and a width of 56 with columns 20 meters high. A **Telamon**, a gigantic male figure, 8 meters high, was found among the ruins. This decorative atlas figure had his arms raised to support the weight of the trabeation. The original is in the Archaeological Museum while the one on site is a reconstruction.

Passing the splendid **Kolymbetra Garden**, an interesting agricultural and historical site with orange trees, acanthus

▼ The 6th century B.C. Temple of Heracles is the oldest.

◄ ▼ The Roman catacombs of Fragapane
and the massive Tomb of Theron built by the Romans.

▼ Telamon, a gigantic atlas figure which supported the trabeation of the Temple of the Olympic Zeus.

▲▶ A hypogeum in the ancient Kolymbetra Garden in the heart of the Valley, with the Temple of the Dioscuri in the background.

plants and terebinth trees, Arab hypogeums and cisterns, one reaches the **Temple of the Dioscuri** or of Castor and Pollux, the twins born of the union of Zeus and Leda queen of Sparta, beloved by the Greeks and Romans. In the 5th century B.C. it was destroyed by the Carthaginians and rebuilt in Greek style and was subsequently destroyed by an earthquake. Thanks to the romantic paintings of the Grand Tour travelers this temple has become an emblem of Agrigento.

Back on the road the next stop is the Church of San Nicola and the Archaeological Museum. The Romanesque-Gothic **Church of San Nicola** overlooks the valley and was built by the Cistercians in the 13th

◀ The Temple of the Dioscuri.

century. It has a portal with a pointed arch. The single nave interior has four chapels. In the second is the richly decorated white marble *Sarcophagus of Phaedra,* a Roman work of the 2nd century B.C. found in the eighteenth century. Next to the church is the 4th century B.C. **Ekklesiasteion** or assembly hall where the citizens met. It is circular and dug into the rock with 22 tiers divided into 5 sectors. The **Archaeological Museum** is behind the church in the former Cistercian convent. Its twenty rooms contain a rich collection of the prehistoric, archaic, Greek and Roman periods with splendid vases, amphoras and Greek kraters of the 6th to 3rd century B.C. In the sixth room is the famous *Telamon* and three other telamon heads as well as the vestiges of the temple of Zeus Olympus. In the tenth room is one of the most famous Greek sculptures: the *Ephebus of Agrigento* of 480 B.C. found in a cistern near the temple of Demeter. This beautiful virile *kouros* was a Greek symbol of youth and devotion to the gods and was therefore installed in the temple courtyard to receive offerings.

▲▶ *Head of a kore,* 5th century B.C. and *head of a telamon,* 5th century B.C. from the Temple of Zeus (Jupiter) (Archaeological Museum).

PELAGIE ISLANDS

▲ Shrine of the Madonna di Porto Salvo in Lampedusa.

Three islands, Lampedusa, Linosa, and Lampione form the archipelago of the Pelagie, from the Greek *Pelaghiè*, or high sea, lying two hundred kilometers from Sicily, with a population of five thousand souls, remote in the midst of the Mediterranean.

These islands differ considerably from each other: Lampedusa almost flat and semi-desert, the largest and best known and most worldly filled with hosts of vacationers in summer; Linosa, the farthest point of Italy fifty-seven kilometers from Lampedusa, mountainous, of volcanic origins, with three extinct craters and figs, prickly pears, vineyards and capers; Lampione, a reef rising sheer from the sea with a lighthouse, and uninhabited. Each one can be a corner of paradise suited to the varying tastes of the visitor. For those who love people and night life, there is Lampedusa where there are parties and bonfires on the beach every night. For those who want to rest in blessed solitude in the midst of nature and the ocean, there is the splendid and solitary Linosa.

The *Caretta Caretta* loggerhead turtles, on the way to extinction, found an ideal place to lay their eggs on the

▼ The sea and the beach of Guitagia in Lampedusa.

beach of the Baia dell'Isola dei Conigli. The rare African striped lizard *Psammodromus algirus*, and the *Columbro cucullato* snake, as well as the monk seals and the queen's falcons, also inhabit this bay.

In antiquity Phoenicians, Greeks and Romans lived here, and then in 813 the Arabs. After centuries of abandon and oblivion, the Pelagie once more came to the fore as penitentiary colonies for the Bourbons. Fascism chose them as a place for political exiles. Everything here is African: from the white light, with a blinding brilliance, to the wind that continuously blows, but that in summer makes the hot African sun easier to support. And then there is the arid semi-desert environment of the interior of Lampedusa, and the cuisine, with *couscous* prepared, unlike the rest of Sicily, with lobster and cherry tomatoes.

LAMPEDUSA is the island that belonged to the noble Tomasi family from 1630 to 1839, the family of Giuseppe Tomasi di Lampedusa who wrote the famous novel "Il Gattopardo" (The Leopard). This island lies at the center of the archipelago with an airport, a small harbor, the town itself consisting of *dammusi*, square white or colored houses, a single street, *Via Roma*, full of small shops, cafes, bars and restaurants.

The around thirty kilometers of coast, in white tufa, are high and jagged, and can only in part be reached on foot. The boat is the best way to discover the grottos, like the one of **Punta Parise**, beaches and spell-binding secluded spots that abound on the island. South of Lampedusa are beaches with fine white sand, with facilities like the one of **Guitagia**, near the harbor and rather crowded, and the famous bays of **Cala Creta**, **Cala Greca**, **Cala Maluk**, and **Cala Croce**, while the fascinating **Cala Pulcino** is a stony fjord. The loveliest bay of Lampedusa, and the most famous in Italy environmentally protected, is the **Baia dei Conigli** opposite the cleef of the same name, candid and solitary, in the midst of a turquoise sea, and connected to the **Isolotto dei Conigli** – the turtle reserve – by a tongue of sand. Lampedusa has no outstanding monuments but the pilgrimage **Shrine of the Madonna di Porto Salvo** is worth a visit.

▼ The lovely renowned Baia dei Conigli with a turquoise sea and favorite haunt of the loggerhead turtles.

◄ ▼ The picturesque colored houses of Linosa and the beach of Cala di Pozzolana with its black rocks.

LINOSA is the small and ancient *Aethusa*, hotter, less windy, with its black lava stone and three craters called Monte Nero, Monte Rosso and Monte Vulcano, but with a flourishing vegetation and fields of lentils, figs, capers, prickly pear and vines, enclosed in geometric gardens with dry-masonry walls. The only way to see Linosa, five square kilometers with a perimeter of one kilometer, is on foot. The charming secrets to be discovered include the tiny town, with its square orange, pink, green and red houses, with brightly colored doors and windows. Linosa is the island for those who want a relaxing vacation, surrounded by nature and the sea. Its black beaches offer spectacular coasts with cliffs plunging straight down into the sea. The beach of **Cala di Pozzolana di Ponente** near the town is dramatic with its black rocks falling sheer to a clear green sea. Small islets between the **Faraglioni** and **Punta Beppe Tuccio** form lagoons where one can swim with not a soul around, while the red and black rocks of **Fili**, rising straight from the sea, conceal a series of grottos that can be reached only by sea. Colonies of seagulls have chosen this site for nesting. Not far from Fili, at **Punta Calcarella**, is the **Sicchitella**, the place scuba divers and snorkelers consider one of the most beautiful and richest in the Mediterranean.

THE UBIQUITOUS PRICKLY PEAR

The succulent tasty prickly pear, yellow, red, green, violet, white (the sweetest one) is the fruit of a rather ugly shapeless plant, stiff and compact, that not even the wind can bend. It is however the symbol of the Sicilian landscape with its curiously exotic aspect. The generous prickly pear, iconography of the island, is found everywhere. It forms hedges along the road, marks the borders of the gardens, and for years has been the bread of the poor – the biblical manna, in subsistence farming – and lastly also as a medicinal plant.

The Sicilian prickly pear or *Opuntia Ficus Indica* is one of the hundred and seventy plants of the *cactus family*. Not only is it ubiquitous, but every part of the plant is used. The pads once pounded and dried furnish fibers that can be woven into mats or baskets. The fruit is nourishing and thirst-quenching, those picked after a rain are like sorbets; dried in the sun they can be used in winter. In some areas of Sicily the prickly pear pads, *nopalitos* when diced, are breaded and fried, while these pads or *cladoesi*, rich in vitamin C, are used as forage, or as ornament, but above all in medicine for they are laxative, cardiotonic, useful in diabetes and gastritis, and to disinfect wounds. The flowers dried in the sun are also used as a diuretic.

Sicilian cuisine has many recipes using the fruit: from syrup to jams and jellies, to cookies, such as the *mostaccioli*. The pickled pears are popular in the countries of Northern Europe. The cochineal insect that feeds on the fruit and pads produces cochineal used as a dye and a basic component of lipstick in the cosmetic field. Montezuma had part of the taxes paid in cochineal.

Florio, the wine producing family, in 1856 installed a firm in Catania for the production of alcohol from the pads of the prickly pear, as did other producers during the Fascist regime. Celebrating it as an "autarchic plant", they also took it to the Italian colonies in Africa.

There is a legend that the prickly pear was introduced to Sicily in secret and as a revenge by the French after the revolt of the co-called Sicilian Vespers in 1282, for they thought the fruit was poisonous. Actually the prickly pear was brought from Mexico by Christopher Columbus in 1495 and introduced into Sicily in the early 16th century by the Spanish rulers together with chocolate. The prickly pear, considered a Christian fruit in the Maghreb, was actually taken to the mid-eastern countries by the Arabs.

CALTANISSETTA

▲ The monumental cemetery in the midst of the countryside of Caltanissetta.

Only two of the many Grand Tour travelers from the north stopped in Caltanissetta in their journeys to discover Italy and Sicily. One was Guy de Maupassant (who visited the mines) and the other was Goethe who defined it as "a desert of fertility" because he was stunned by the fields of wheat. This is the land of the sulphur deposits, with mines of rock salt, sulphur and potassium salts, of large landed estates and feuds, where the powerful Sicilian nobility lived, in a monochromatic yellow landscape of wheat, sun and sulphur. Located between Agrigento and Enna, Caltanissetta is the focal point of the sulphur bearing plateau, and the mine has left a profound mark on the city, the people, to the point of modifying their life. At the beginning of the nineteenth century these lands, at the zenith of their mining and economic wealth, were the setting for bitter struggles and strikes by the peasants and miners against the powerful owners of the landed estates and the subsoil, in their attempts to obtain better conditions of life. These struggles, as narrated by the writer Leonardo Sciascia who was born among the sulphur deposits of Racalmuto, and the brutality of work in the mines were what finally led the Sicilian man to an awareness of himself as a person. The mines, closed a score of years ago because of American competition, produced four-fifths of the world's sulphur. Today Caltanissetta is concentrating on tourism, cultural and not, in the mining areas, thanks to the ethno-anthropological museums, evocative parks of industrial archaeology. The city boasts of a series of folklore festivals that begin in spring and have their roots in the Spanish domination. The most important event is Holy Week with a spectacular procession. The climax is reached on Holy Saturday, with the *Scinnenza*, the deposition of Christ, when the people in choir, accompanied by the band, sing the sweet sad dirge of the *Ladi* in an archaic dialect. *Piazza Garibaldi* in Caltanissetta with its **Triton Fountain** is the heart of the city, behind a ray of lanes and alleys, where Middle Ages and Baroque intermingle and where the two most important streets cross: *Corso Umberto* and *Corso Vittorio Emanuele*. The Cathedral and the Church of San Sebastiano overlook the piazza. The **Cathedral** is dedicated to Santa Maria La Nova and to

▼ The Cathedral of Santa Maria la Nova and Raphael's *Spasimo di Sicilia* (copy), in the Diocesan Museum.

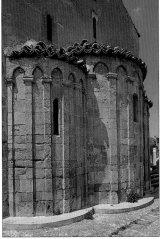

Saint Michael. The church with its neoclassic facade was built between 1570 and 1622 and is flanked by two nineteenth-century bell towers. The nave is decorated with stuccoes and eighteenth-century frescoes by the Flemish painter Guglielmo Borremans. An *Immaculate Conception*, the *Coronation of the Virgin*, and a *Triumph of Saint Michael* dominate the barrel vault. Another fine work by Borremans is in the sanctuary, on the high altar: an altarpiece of the *Immacolata and Saints*. The organ with a seventeenth-century chancel is wonderfully elegant. In the **Diocesan Museum** is a copy of Raphael's famous painting, the *Spasimo di Sicilia*, the original of which is in the Prado in Madrid. Opposite the Cathedral is the sixteenth-century **Church of San Sebastiano**, the saint who is said to have freed the city from the plague. At the corner of the piazza is the **Town Hall** built on the old Church of Maria SS. Annunziata. Along the street are various monumental noble residences, **Palazzo Giordano**, **Palazzo Candelotti**, **Palazzo Bordonaro**, up to the **Church** and **College of Sant'Agata**, an elegant and original structure with red plasterwork. It has a wealth of decorations and polychrome marble inlays, and frescoes by Luigi Borremans. The altarpiece by Agostino Scilla on the high altar with the *Martyrdom of Saint Agatha* is splendid and just as fine is the marble altar frontal depicting *Saint Ignatius in Glory*, by Ignazio Marabitti, in the left transept.

Crossing the medieval quarter of the Angeli, after the **Church of San Domenico**, decorated with stuccoes and paintings by Filippo Paladino, one comes to the cliff with the ruins of the **Castle of Pietrarossa**, called *murra di l'Ancili* by the inhabitants, an Arab construction, later a Norman fortress. Frederick II of Aragon was proclaimed king here. The castle collapsed, probably because of an earthquake.

Finds (vases, utensils) from the necropolises in the area around the city are in the **Archaeological Museum**. The **Museum of Mineralogy and of the Zolfara** is in the Institute of Mineralogy and has collections of fossils and rare rocks. The sulphur and gypsum crystals are as beautiful as gems.

Three kilometers from Caltanissetta is one of the oldest and most representative monuments of the city: the eleventh-century **Abbey of Santo Spirito**, a Romanesque church with three apses founded by Count Roger and his wife Adelasia. The walls inside are frescoed and a seventeenth-century *Crucifix* by the artist Salvo d'Antonio is over a splendid Romanesque baptismal font.

The **archaeological site of Sabucina**, on a hill, is eight kilometers from the city. It has prehistoric circular huts, Bronze Age necropolis, parts of Greek walls and dwellings dating to the 7th and 6th century B.C.

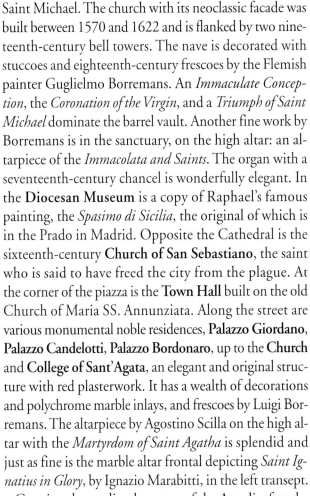

▶ The facade of the Church of San Sebastiano.

ENNA

▲▼ The splendid fertile countryside of Enna.

The city that Cicero called *Umbelicus Siciliae*, the navel of Italy, Enna, is in the heart of Sicily. Located at an altitude of nine hundred and forty-three meters on terracing that overlooks the Erei Mountains, the valleys of the Salso and Simeto, Enna is also called the "viewpoint of Sicily". The highest capital in Italy, Enna keeps to itself, guarding its traditions and customs with rhythms that still follow the alternating seasons. History passed through this city called invincible but dominated by one civilization after the other. In antiquity it was the center of the cult of Ceres, the goddess of harvests, to whom a temple was erected. Much of its economy is still based on agriculture, with almonds, cereals and olives, in defiance of the harsh sulphurous Sicilian earth. The spectacle in spring when the flowering almonds cover the hills in a mantle of white is superb. Enna is the cradle of ancient baronial holdings and is in an area of sulphur deposits (the sulphur triangle is Enna, Caltanissetta and Agrigento). After World War II the countryside was rent by bitter peasant and mining revolts.

The city, of prehistoric foundations, was home to Siculi and Sicani. It was the granary of Rome and nourished the Roman plebe and when the magistrate Gaius Licinius Verre raided and plundered the temple of the goddess and removed the great statues of Ceres and Triptolemos, the people raised such an uproar that the Ro-

man senate sent a commission headed by Cicero to investigate. He supported the citizens and condemned Verre. Then came the Byzantines and the Arabs who filled it with plants, flowers and new crops and created irrigation canals.

Two events mobilize the entire city of Enna: the *feast of the patron Maria Santissima della Visitazione* on July 2, with the rite of the transport of the wagon of Ceres, and then *Holy Week*.

The city has kept its historical center, still Arab, intact, with its tangle of streets and the houses piled up one on the other. The **Castle of Lombardia**, one of the most important in Sicily, twenty-six thousand square meters, is on the southeastern edge on an outcrop of rock. It was built for Frederick II of Swabia in 1100 on an Arab fortress, in a pentagonal plan with powerful walls and twenty square lookout towers of which only six are still standing. Inside the castle are a small church, the emperor's apartments and a series of courtyards one after the other.

◀ Bas-relief with *Saint Martin and the poor man* on the portal of the Cathedral.

One of these leads to the famous keep, the **Torre Pisana** (Pisan Tower), or **of Frederick**, with its crenellations, offering a splendid panorama of the valleys and Mount Etna. Not far from the castle are the ruins of the **Rocca di Cerere**, the Fortress of Ceres, on a sheer cliff.

On the opposite side of the city is another imposing structure, the octagonal **Frederick's Tower**, twenty-four meters high, and probably the emperor's residence.

The **Cathedral** of Enna is a vertical building of 1307, erected in honor of the Virgin Mother, for Eleonor, wife of Ferdinand II. Destroyed by fire in 1446 it was rebuilt. A fine sixteenth-century portal, the tympanum decorated with a marble bas-relief depicting *Saint Martin*

◀ ▼ The Pisan Tower or of Frederick and the imposing Castle of Lombardia.

▲ ▶ Archaeological finds in the Museum of Enna in Palazzo Varisano.

Museum, in **Palazzo Varisano**, are tomb furnishings dating to the third and second millennium B.C. from the necropolises in the territory of Enna.

The **Lake of Pergusa** celebrated by Ovid in the *Metamorphoses* is only nine kilometers from Enna. It was here that Hades, the god of the Underworld, abducted Proserpina (Kore or Persephone). The eucalyptus grove on the shores of the lake hides an enormous cave, the mythical cavern where Hades took the maiden. This is the first place the more romantic tourist visits.

and the poor man, leads into the Latin-cross three-aisled interior. The Baroque basilica is decorated with statues, paintings, black basalt columns with extravagant figure ornamentation. The fifteenth-century statue of the patron saint of Enna, the *Madonna of the Visitation*, in a golden *fercolo* or litter, is in the right aisle, as is the fine painting of the *Visitation* by Filippo Paladino.

The church **Treasury** is in the **Alessi Museum**, which also contains a precious collection of coins, candelabra and monstrances in solid silver, and the famous golden Crown of the Madonna of 1653, studded with diamonds, precious stones and enamels. Opposite, in the **Archaeological**

Half-way between Enna and Piazza Armerina is the archaeological site of the ancient **MORGANTINA**, surrounded by olives and vineyards. The city was founded in 850 B.C. by the Morgeti, an Italic tribe. Of note is the **Agora**, a rectangular raised area with fourteen tiers on which the people sat in assembly. Lower down is the fourth-century B.C. **Theater**, set against the hill, and nearby the **House of Ganymede** named after the 3rd century B.C. mosaic depicting the abduction of the youth.

◀ ▼ The Agora and the mosaics of Morgantina.

GELA

▲▼ *Giummare*, dwarf palms that grow in Gela and the splendid beaches of Licata.

Gela is on the southern coast of Sicily, bathed by the African sea, with beaches of golden sand and dunes, a fertile plain, the land of "*giummare*" (dwarf palms). It has a nature park, the *Biviere di Gela*, and an important archaeological site, the fruit of a great and glorious past, while the present is marked by a rather forced industrialization, the result of unfulfilled promises and unauthorised building. Gela was a powerful and cultured Greek city. The first Dorian colony in Sicily, its coinage was recognized throughout the Greek world. The center of arts and letters, Aeschylus the tragedian died here. In the 5th century B.C. it was governed by Hippocrates who was succeeded by Gelon, and the capital was moved to Syracuse. A hundred years after its birth (669 B.C.) it in turn founded the city of *Akragas* (Agrigento). Its fate, like its history, is that of decline and rebirth, greatness and misery. In 405 B.C. Gela fell for the first time to the Carthaginians who destroyed it. It rose up again and in 282 B.C. fell under the tyrant of Agrigento Phintias who razed it to the ground. In 1232 Frederick II reconstructed it on archaic Gela and called it Heraclea. Later, until 1927, it was known as Terranova. Between 1370 and 1390 it fell into the hands of pirates from North Africa. In the 18th century it rose again, to fall once more, until the euphoria of the discovery of oil in 1956 led to the birth of the oil industry, which so far however has not led to the hoped for wealth and well-being.

Gela today is known for its archaeological site, near which are derricks, pylons and black chimney stacks. Myth and beauty sit side by side with the signs of the petrochemical industry. The splendid museum and the ruins, eloquent signs of its past, however make a visit to Gela more than worthwhile. The **Archaeological Museum**

contains four thousand items, including finds of artefacts, masks, sarcophagi. The figurines of *Demeter and Athena* testifying to the rebirth of Gela in the 3rd century B.C. are magnificent, as is the small clay figure of the *Kore* bearing an incense burner on her head (6th century B.C.). Parts of the wreck of a Greek ship found in the waters of Gela are also in the museum, with its load of vases, kraters, Punic, Corinthian and Attic amphoras and ceremonial objects (small clay altars, a bronze tripod and a small simulacrum consecrated to Athena). Not far from Gela on the highest part of the hill is the **Acropolis**, with the remains of two Doric temples, part of the sacred precinct of Athena. The first, archaic, dates to the 6th century B.C., the second to the 5th century. A **plateia** separates the acropolis into two zones, north and south. In the former are the remains of houses, shops, and portions of sixth-century B.C. walls,

◀ ▼ Fifth century B.C. antefix and terra cotta sixth century B.C. statuette in the Archaeological Museum.

while the southern area was used for cultural activities. Fragments of **Greek fortifications** can be seen at Capo Soprano, another archaeological site west of the town: a stretch of stone and brick wall, three hundred meters long, that protected the city. It is an evocative site and the panorama of the sea can be enjoyed while wandering through the ruins. Not far off are the **Hellenistic public baths**, the only Greek baths discovered in Sicily, with fine terracotta tubs with seats dating to the 4th century B.C.

◀ ▼ View of the Acropolis of Gela and the solitary column, all that remains of the Doric Temple.

AN AGE-OLD SCOURGE OFFENDING THE ISLAND

A picture of the beauty and prosperity of this large island cannot ignore the age-old scourge of the mafia, the presence of organized crime that dates back to over a hundred years ago and is also known as Cosa Nostra. Basically this scourge is due to the disregard for the State that exists in some levels of Sicilian society, an attitude of tacit complicity as a result of the historical neglect of the island by the State. What it all adds up to is a perverse tangle of criminality, business and politics that leads to extortion, protection money, drug dealing, with recurrent ferocious crimes between organized crime syndicates or against those who are fighting them in the name of the law. It must be added that hosts of heroic magistrates have been fighting the mafia and many have paid for their tireless and perilous attempts at justice with their lives. Some of these judges have become emblems of courage and of the Sicilian recovery, such as Giovanni Falcone (killed in an explosion in May 1992) and Paolo Borsellino killed in the same way, together with five of his escort, barely fifty-seven days after Falcone. The long list of intrepid magistrates includes Caponnetto, Rocco Chinnici, Piero Grasso, prosecutor in Palermo, to which must be added the task undertaken by the Antimafia Commission and recently embodied in the judge Pier Luigi Vigna. Many of Leonardo Sciascia's writings take the form of documents analyzing mafia society and temperament, in an effort to explain the origins of the phenomenon, that goes back to even before the unification of Italy, but also aware of the hopes many Sicilians nurture in their hearts.

The deep-rooted age-old phenomenon of the mafia has little to do with the temperament and courage of the overwhelming majority of the Sicilians, a talented hard working people who are often the victims. The constant growth in the modernization of the island, the reclamation of the persistent pockets of misery and ignorance, major transparency in administration and business (especially in the contracts for great public works), together with the fight carried out by the State and the courageous magistrates on site, lead one to believe that the future of the mafia cannot keep pace with the present.

▲▼ Playbill of the film "The Godfather" with Marlon Brando and the Courthouse in Palermo.

CALTAGIRONE

▲▼ Statuettes in the Ceramic Museum and panorama of Caltagirone.

Caltagirone is a city that scintillates with the colors of its ceramic tiles (blue, green and yellow) decorating staircases, gardens, balconies and frontages. The spectacular Baroque churches and convents together with the ubiquitous tiles make it one of the most singular of Sicilian cities.

Ceramics for Caltagirone are history, culture and the principal economic resource, as well as the symbol of Sicily. There are more than a hundred and sixty workshops, and more than a thousand craftsmen in a population of thirty thousand. Shops, galleries and workshops with the *"cannatari"* artisans (from *cannate*, or jug) shaping the clay on the potter's wheel line the long staircase of Santa Maria del Monte. Caltagirone has rendered tribute to its majolicas by opening the *Istituto d'Arte* to train aspiring potters, and with the **Ceramic Museum** in the public park, known as la Villa, in Italy surpassed only by the one in Faenza. The museum contains objects that narrate the story of Sicilian ceramics from prehistory to the present. Caltagirone owes its fame and wealth to the abun-

dance of clay in its territory, and prehistoric kilns found in **Contrada San Mauro** bear witness this age-old activity. The Greeks continued. The Cretans brought the potter's wheel and production became more efficient. Un-

◄ ▲ A potter at work and the typical ceramics of Caltagirone.

der Arab domination in the 10th century glazing techniques and new patterns and colors were introduced, yellow, green and blue with geometric designs and stylized animals and plants. The Arabs were driven out on July 25, 1090 and the city was conquered by the Normans of Count Roger aided by the Genoese Giorgio Maniace. The *festa di San Giacomo* celebrates this event every year with the illumination of the Stairs of Santa Maria del Monte with four thousand colored lamps carpeting the whole stairway.

With the advent of Spanish domination, the Moorish-Catalan taste prevailed and blue became the prevalent color. The traditional vases, amphoras, *albarello* pharmaceutical jars and whistles go hand in hand with the production of Nativity figurines and tiles to decorate cupolas, palaces and balconies, as well as effigies of saints, particularly popular after the earthquake of January 11, 1693 which wiped out entire quarters. Caltagirone, like many Sicilian cities, was built in the Baroque style, without however compromising the original medieval layout with its tangle of steep

winding paved lanes and alleys, with staircases and widenings called "*carruggi*" as in Genoa by the Ligurians who lived there, a name that is still used.

▶ Majolica panel in the Ceramic Museum.

Baroque palaces. **Palazzo Bellaprima**, the town hall, and **Palazzo Senatorio**, dating to 1483 and now the premises of the *Galleria d'Arte Don Sturzo*, are on *Piazza del Municipio*, once Piano della Loggia, where the two streets cross. The famous **Staircase of Santa Maria del Monte** of 1608 with a rise of 50 meters and 142 lava stair treads is near the piazza. In 1954 the stairs were decorated with majolica tiles in a compendium of Arab, Norman and Spanish styles by Antonio Ragona. Four thousand colored lamps are set on the steps for the *festa di San Giacomo*, or feast of Saint James, creating an unforgettable spectacle. At the top overlooking the city is the **Chiesa Matrice di Santa Maria del Monte**, twelfth

Luigi Sturzo, a priest and an important figure in Italian politics who founded the Partito Popolare Italiano in 1919, was born in Caltagirone. It was thanks to this party, later transformed into the Christian Democrat party, that the Catholics entered politics after the Risorgimento. For thirteen years Don Luigi Sturzo was mayor of Caltagirone and he founded the Istituto d'Arte della Ceramica in the city.

The city is divided into two parts: the upper part, the old heart of the town, and the lower part, with the staircase of Santa Maria del Monte and two main streets, *Corso Vittorio Emanuele* and *Via Roma* connecting the two. The upper part is characterized by splendid aristocratic ocher-colored

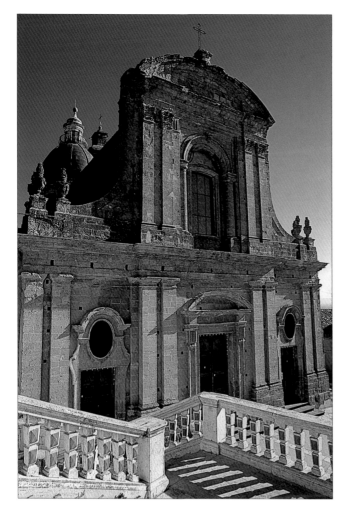

◀ ▲ The Chiesa Matrice di Santa Maria del Monte and the majolica balustrade of Palazzo Ventimiglia.

century but transformed in the sixteenth and rebuilt after the earthquake of 1603, with an eighteenth-century bell tower. The three aisled interior has a Byzantine panel painting with the *Conadomini Madonna* on the high altar and, to the right of the choir, a work by Domenico Gagini, the *Madonna della Purificazione*.

Near Piazza del Municipio, the **Corte Capitaniale** and the Cathedral are in Piazza Umberto I. The former is an old court building of 1601. The **Cathedral**, a blend of various architectural styles, was never finished. The facade dates to 1909 and the bell tower to 1954. Descending Via Roma, a street opened in 1766, towards the lower

city one encounters the semicircular construction faced with majolica tiles and with an *eagle* on the top, the standard of Caltagirone, known as **Tondo Vecchio**. After the public park – known as la **Villa** – is the eighteenth-century **Balaustra Ventimiglia**. This is the most photographed terrace, completely faced with polychrome majolica tiles by the great majolica artist Benedetto Ventimiglia. Before leaving Caltagirone, visit the **Church of San Giorgio** in Via Sturzo in the old Arab quarter.

▶ The tile-covered "Tondo Vecchio".

PIAZZA ARMERINA

Piazza Armerina is a charming town located in one of the most fertile parts of Sicily, in the midst of a landscape of orchards, almond and olive trees, eucalyptus and pine woods, and water. Built on three hills, it is known throughout the world for its famous Villa of Casale and the mosaics defined as "the eighth marvel of archaeology". Greeks, Arabs, Normans and Spaniards all left signs of their passage here, in palaces, castles, churches and convents.

Every year on August 15th for the feast of the patron saint of the city, Santa Maria delle Vittorie, the *Palio dei Normanni*, a historical cavalcade reenacting the triumphant entrance into the city of Count Roger de Hauteville in 1087 with the image of the Madonna, is held.

The center of Piazza Armerina is *Piazza Garibaldi* with its trees and gardens and the point of departure for the

▼ Panorama of the city.

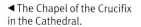

◄ The Chapel of the Crucifix in the Cathedral.

tangle of streets, lanes and alleyways, with old dilapidated houses, courtyards and staircases, aristocratic palaces, churches, shops, bars and restaurants.

The **Cathedral**, the most important monument in the city, is dedicated to Our Lady of the Assumption. Built in 1627 on a fifteenth-century church, the dome dates to 1768, and there is a bell tower with two fine pairs of Gothic-Catalan windows. It was built for the powerful baron Marco Trigona to designs by the architect Orazio Torrioni. In the blue and white interior the Byzantine icon of the *Madonna delle Vittorie*, a gift of Pope Nicholas II to Count Roger de Hauteville, is on the high altar. There is also a splendid wooden *Cross* of 1485, painted on both sides, in the chapel to the left of the presbytery, and the *Assumption of the Virgin*, a painting by Filippo Paladino. Of particular note are the inlaid wooden choir stalls. Opposite the Cathedral is the lavish Baroque **Palazzo Trigona Canicarao**, with a wealth of fine windows and balconies. Not far off are the imposing ruins of the fourteenth-century **Aragonese Castle**, a powerful square structure with imposing towers. The **Church of the Priorato di Sant'Andrea**, a Romanesque twelfth-century gem, stands along the road that leads to the Roman ruins of Villa of Casale.

The famous **Roman Villa of Casale** of the 3rd century A.D., five kilometers from the historical center, and declared a World Heritage Site by UNESCO, is the most important Roman archaeological park in Sicily. The luxurious and splendid rural residence, with forty rooms in four separate buildings connected to each other by courtyards, corridors and doors, was built on terraces in a softly rolling green valley, probably on the old city of *Philosophiana*. It belonged to a certain Procopius Populonius, who imported wild animals from Africa for the amphitheater games in Rome. Some however maintain that the owner of the Villa was Maximianus Herculius,

► Columns in the Atrium of the Villa of Casale.

▲ ◄ The *triclinium* and a mosaic depicting "Autumn" in the Room of the Four Seasons.

one of the tetrarchs who ruled the empire in A.D. 286-305 and was forced by Diocletian to abdicate. Whoever it was, he loved beauty and luxury, and certain oriental sensual delights as revealed in the mosaics. By some the style and subjects of these third-century mosaics are considered reminiscent of Carthage. In the course of the centuries the pagan Villa fell into ruin, but 3,500 square meters of the mosaic floor were saved and are rightly considered some of the finest in the world, both in size and charm. Two aqueducts have been discovered outside the villa which provided water for the fountains, baths and services. A series of footways along a fixed route take one into the villa from a courtyard that leads to a polygonal **atrium** with a fountain at the center.

▲ Mosaic in the vestibule of the Small Circus.

◀▲ The Corridor of the Great Hunt and close-up of "Africa" in a lunette.

The **frigidarium** is an octagonal bath with mosaics of marine scenes: tritons, cupids and charming nereids while the **tepidarium** and the three **calidaria** have lost their floor mosaics even though the layout for the circulation of hot air can still be identified. The **peristyle** is reached from a room, perhaps the **palaestra**, with splendid mosaics of quadriga races. In the **vestibule** is a mosaic depicting a servant welcoming guests with an olive branch. Rooms to the

▲ *Diaeta* of the Small Hunt.

▼ ► The famous mosaic of *Girls in bikinis* and an *erotic scene* in the Cubicle of Love.

▼ ► The famous mosaic of *Girls in bikinis* and an *erotic scene* in the Cubicle of Love.

left of the peristyle are decorated with mosaics of birds, cupids and flowers, perhaps the children's rooms and others, with geometric patterns. The most interesting is the **Room of the Small Hunt** with a mosaic with scenes of the hunt and banquets. The long **Corridor of the Great Hunt** has African influences and charm, with sixty meters of fine brightly colored mosaics depicting men hunting wild animals, boar, elephants, a rhinoceros. Other mosaics portray Africa and Asia, perhaps in homage to the generous host who owned the villa. The corridor led to the private part of the villa with the apartments: a **vestibule** with the mosaics of *Ulysses* and *Polyphemus*, the **cubicle** with an erotic scene, two **apsed rooms**, and the **Room of Arion**, where the mosaics depict *Arion astride a dolphin*. Other rooms follow, all with mosaics, up to the famous **Room of the Girls in Bikinis**, which have cap-

tured the public imagination because the costumes of the ten gymnasts, or *palestrite*, look surprisingly like bikinis. An elliptical peristyle leads to the **triclinium**, the dining room of the opulent villa.

RAGUSA

◀ ▲ ▼ Carob tree and carob beans grown in the province of Ragusa and view of Ragusa Ibla.

To reach Ragusa, a city on a rocky plateau of the Ibla mountains, one passes through a varying landscape of almond trees, age-old olives, carobs, prickly pears, fields of broad beans and wheat.

Since 1963 crude oil has been extracted here and the metal derricks, together with the bell towers of the churches, mark the silhouette of the city. Crude oil however has not brought the dreamed of riches nor solved the infinite problems, and agriculture, the land, is still the principal source of income in this province where emphyteusis, a real agricultural revolution, was practiced by the feudal landlords, favored by the Count Cabrera in 1452, which meant that the peasant cultivated his piece of land directly, which be- came his in exchange for the payment of rent, although his title to the land was still subject to the needs of the landlord. The peasant origins of Ragusa, and the entire territory, are evident in the cuisine, in the tasty chick pea and broad bean soups, in the wheat, the roast lamb and

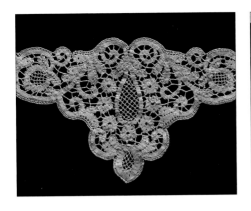

▲ Sicilian *sfilato* lace and the typical *caciocavallo* cheese of Ragusa.

The discovery of Ragusa begins with Ibla, stretching out at the base of the great rocky spur that in antiquity was the first colony of the Greeks of Syracuse, then the Byzantines, Arabs, Normans, and eventually the domain of the Counts Cabrera who advocated emphyteusis (see above).

Wandering through the tangle of streets and looking upwards often at the infinite curlicues, garlands, cherubs and allegorical figures in stone that decorate the buildings, not infrequently women will be encountered seated along the street embroidering or making lace, with on their laps the *tombolo*, the typical oval padded frame with bobbins and threads which are skillfully interlaced and knotted to create *sfilato siciliano* lace. These marvelous laces have always decorated the superb trousseaus of the aristocratic women, church altars and vestments.

Ragusa Ibla is in white tufa, with the imposing Baroque

couscous, in DOC cheeses such as *caciocavallo*, the vaunt of the citizens, and the excellent butter, still churned by hand in the small dairies. The area is known also for its honey, golden, flavorful and fragrant, particularly carob and thyme honey, produced in antiquity by the Greeks and extolled by their poets. Just as sweet, like nectar, is the *Ambrato di Comiso* (a neighboring locality), a wine that marks the end of every meal and that is also drunk throughout the day.

After the earthquake of 1693 that destroyed half of southern Sicily, Ragusa was divided into two parts: the lower city, Ragusa Ibla, and Ragusa Alta. The old city is in the lower part, stubbornly rebuilt in its medieval layout with houses set one on top of the other, connected by staircases, vaulting, lanes, and alleys.

Ragusa Alta was created by the noble land owners and the Church in the style of the time, the Baroque, and has a wealth of churches, convents, palaces, staircases, as well as industries and viaducts that connect the various quarters. A stairway of two hundred and forty-two steps and *Corso Mazzini*, a zigzag street created under Fascism, connect the two Ragusas. In 1926 Fascism put an end to the parochialism by unifying the two cities. Ragusa Ibla is the more fascinating, and entranced Pietro Germi who set his film "Divorzio all'italiana" (Divorce Italian Style) with Marcello Mastroianni and Stefania Sandrelli in this out of the way city.

Ragusa is in the southeastern corner of Sicily, for the Arabs the Val di Noto, where the 1693 earthquake did most damage.

When there is work, it is still agriculture that marks the rhythms of time, life, and the rites in the festivals connected with rural activities. The Sicilians here are different: quieter and more introverted, but kind, generous and ceremonious.

▶ Ragusa Ibla from Santa Maria delle Scale.

The **Church of the Cappuccini Vecchi**, with paintings by Pietro Novelli, is in the public park **Giardino Ibleo** with a fine panorama of the valley. The **Church of San Giorgio Vecchio** was almost completely destroyed by the earthquake but still has its splendid Gothic portal, with *Saint George killing the dragon* and the *Aragonese eagle* in the lunette.

Cathedral dedicated to Saint George on high. It was built between 1738 and 1775 to designs by the brilliant eighteenth-century Syracusan architect Rosario Gagliardi. Highly scenic, it stands at the top of a monumental staircase in a downward sloping piazza that makes it look even taller. The sumptuous three-tiered facade is decorated with superimposed bands of columns and is narrow and convex in the central part, in a play of lights and shadows, with a nineteenth-century dome. There are paintings of note inside.

The nineteenth-century building known as **Circolo di Conversazione**, where the notables and aristocrats once met, overlooks Piazza del Duomo. Inside there are original stuccoes, gilded mirrors and red velvet. All around is a splendid setting of elegant patrician palaces, with bulging balconies, wrought-iron railings and sculptured allegorical figures.

▶ The sumptuous Baroque of the Cathedral of San Giorgio in Ragusa Ibla.

◀ Panorama of the city from Santa Maria delle Scale.

century, consecrated to Saint John the Baptist. The church is built on a porticoed suspended terrace and has a bell tower. The solemn portal is decorated with fluted columns and Corinthian capitals. The interior of the three-aisled Latin-cross Cathedral is a marvel of curlicues and laces in stucco, polychrome marbles, and frescoes, all testifying to the will of Ragusa to rise up from the ashes, as well as the symbol of the wealth of the land-owning aristocracy.

Numerous prehistoric finds, ceramics, Greek sculpture and objects in clay from the necropolises in the environs, as well as splendid mosaics, are in the **Museo Archeologico Ibleo** (Hyblaean Archaeological Museum), in the Palazzo Mediterraneo), recently enlarged.

One of the places that has to be seen on leaving Ragusa and heading for the sea is Modica (thirty kilometers from Ragusa).

At the top of the spectacular monumental **stairway** that connects the two Ragusas is the magnificent fourteenth-century **Church of Maria delle Scale**, built on the ruins of a Norman church of which it still has the portal. Ragusa Alta has a checkerboard layout of streets and piazzas, centered on *Corso Italia* and *Via Vittorio Veneto*, the two main streets. Behind the latter is the **Cathedral**, 18th

◀ ▼ The Church of Purgatory in Ragusa Ibla and the cathedral of San Giovanni Battista in Ragusa Alta.

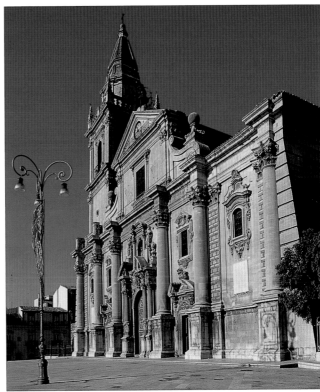

A BIT OF CHOCOLATE

"To be eaten in squares or melted in a cup, of incomparable flavor"...This is what Leonardo Sciascia had to say of the chocolate of Modica, processed for four centuries with the same love and methods of the ancient Aztecs from whom the Spanish conquistadors of Hernán Cortés – the first to drink it at the court of the emperor Montezuma – wrested the lands, the seeds and secrets of the *xocoàtl* and spread them throughout Europe. The Aragonese brought the chocolate beans as gift to the Countship of Modica as a reward for its fidelity. It was a missionary friar, Bernardino da Sahagun, who taught the citizens of Modica how to prepare solid chocolate and the antique recipe has been handed down from generation to generation and still survives. The secret of this exquisite chocolate extolled throughout the world is in its artisan technique of cold working.

Together with aromatic chocolate (also furnished today by industries), Modica produces several other varieties, using citrus peel, as well as *torroni* and other traditional sweets. The production is also exported.

In a population of barely fifty thousand, Modica has nineteen chocolate shops, pastry shops and bakeries, some historical such as the *Antica Dolceria Bonajuto* (dating to 1880) and the *Dolceria Spinello*, with-

▲ The old Dolceria Bonajuto.

out counting the workshops and small family shops that the city has united in the I.G.P. consortium to safeguard this extraordinary chocolate made without vegetable oils and in demand throughout the world.

The Arabs introduced the Sicilians to sugar and the sweet excesses of the *torroni*, *pasta reale* and honey, considered *xocoàtl*, a real food, an energetic that could alleviate fatigue, and the substantial and tasty *'npanitigghi* (puff pastry filled with meat, or eggplant, with cinnamon, chocolate and almonds, rather like the Spanish *empanaditas*) were food for the poorer classes and were also used by the Spanish sailors. The Spanish were the first to mix cocoa and sugar. They also added the Baroque taste for spices they so dearly loved. This is where the figure of the **ciucculattaru** originated, a man with a cart who went from house to house selling chocolate prepared on the spot by grinding the cocoa beans on the *metate* (the concave Aztec millstone), adding sugar, and there was your espresso chocolate.

◄ The exquisite chocolate sweets made by the Dolceria Spinello.

MODICA

Modica, was the countship of the powerful Gattopardi families, who became particularly important under the viceroys and of whom the Sicilian Federico De Roberto gives an extraordinary picture in his classic novel "The Viceroys". Modica is a delightful town with ancient origins: from the Siculi who called it *Motyka* to the Arabs who called it *Mohac*. After the Norman domination it became one of the richest and most powerful countships in Sicily.

Modica is famous not only for the splendid Baroque of its hundred churches, convents and palaces (declared World Heritage Site by UNESCO, like other cities in the area of Ragusa) but also because of the chocolate brought there by the Spanish after the discovery of the new world.

In Modica, like Ragusa, a staircase, a street and three bridges (one of which is the highest in Europe) join the two parts of the city, *in the form of a split pomegranate*, to which the Sicilian writer Gesualdo Bufalino, born in nearby Comiso, has dedicated lovely pages in his book "*Blind Argus*". Modica also has another famous son, the poet Salvatore Quasimodo, Nobel Prize in 1959, one of the most important figures of Italian Hermetism, who translated the Greek classics and published collections of poetry such as, "*Ed è subito sera*", "*La vita non è un sogno*" (Life is not a Dream). His house, at the top of a flight of steps in Via Posterla, can be visited and has a small museum inside.

In the midst of the convents and aristocratic palaces laden with inlays, figures, statues and balconies, there are two particularly noteworthy churches: the Chiesa Madre di San Giorgio, and the Church of Santa Maria di Betlemme.

▼ Panorama of the city
with the Church of San Pietro in the foreground.

The **Chiesa Madre di San Giorgio** (the Cathedral of Modica Alta) was rebuilt by Rosario Gagliardi, a Syracusan architect, who experimented with original scenic Baroque solutions in reconstructing the damaged earthquake zones. The Cathedral of Modica, reaching to the sky, is considered the absolute masterpiece and summa of the prodigious Sicilian Baroque architecture. A monumental staircase of two hundred and fifty steps leads up to the facade with its three levels and single bell tower. The interior with a nave and double side aisles has a wealth of precious decorative details and a polyptych of 1573 with the *Story of Saint George*, by Bernardino Niger, and a splendid chased silver altar. The chapel to the left of the sanctuary contains the statue of the *Madonna of the Snows* (1510)

◀ ▲ The Baroque Cathedral of San Giorgio and detail of the facade, masterpiece by Rosario Gagliardi.

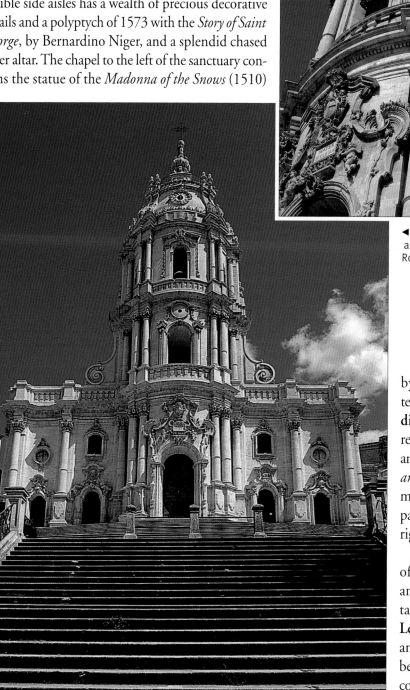

by Bartolomeo Berrettaro. The fifteenth-century **Church of Santa Maria di Betlemme**, in Modica Bassa, was rebuilt after 1693 and has three aisles and a trussed roof. There is a *Madonna and Child* in the Cappella del Sacramento while the *Nativity scene* in painted terracotta in the chapel to the right of the altar dates to 1882.

Little remains of the various **Castles** of the noble Chiaramonte, Cabrera and Naselli families, but monumental buildings such as the **Palazzo De Leva** or **Palazzo Manenti** with figures and masks sculptured below the pot-bellied elegant balustrades can be encountered along the main street *Corso Umberto* where the Jews had their quarter up to 1474.

◀ ▲ Byzantine fresco in the Hypogeum of San Michele and the necropolis of Parco della Forza at Cava d'Ispica.

An outing from Modica (eight kilometers) through carobs and olives, leads to **CAVA D'ISPICA**, not to be missed, with its **prehistoric** and **rock necropolis** in the grottos of the plateau. Eroded by the rivers, these grottos are known as "*cave*" or quarries, and stretch out for twelve kilometers. Some later became Byzantine churches, such as the **Hypogeum of San Michele** which still has fine mural drawings and a fresco with the *Madonna*.

Not far from here, where the Sicilian coast faces Africa across the sea, in the midst of the extraordinary **Riserva di Vendicari** is **POZZALLO**, a seaside town, resort and maritime landing place dominated by a fourteenth-century tower. Pozzallo was the birthplace of Giorgio La Pira (1904-1977), an internationally known figure who is in the process of being proclaimed a saint. La Pira was the lawmaker who collaborated in the drawing up of the Constitution of the Republic of Italy, was deputy in Parliament, and mayor of Florence, his adopted city, for a dozen years, but above all he was an intrepid man of faith who ceaselessly defended peace in the world. His trips and meetings with great men from Ben-Gurion to Nasser, Khrushchev to Ho Chi Minh at the time of the Cold War were legendary.

In 2004, the centennial of his birth, important events and meetings dedicated to him took place in Pozzallo, Rome and Florence, while his many works are now being published.

▶ Park in the Nature Sanctuary of Vendicari.

THAT PRODIGIOUS BAROQUE

Sicilian art is known for its Baroque style, above all in those parts of the region where so many of the buildings were razed to the ground in the earthquake of 1693 and then rebuilt in Baroque style with an admixture of neoclassic. The Baroque began in Rome in the early seventeenth century with Bernini and Borromini, and developed in different ways, ending up in the multiform and multicolored Sicilian Baroque. Typical of Baroque in general and of the Sicilian in particular is the blending of architecture and surroundings, scenography and perspective, almost as if it were a movie set.

Visitors to these cities, pearls of architecture, Noto (called a "garden of stone"), Modica, Ragusa, Syracuse, Catania and Palermo, are soon overwhelmed by this play of forms and colors. This Baroque is characterized by a continuous play of light, of full and empty spaces, of dynamic visions and perspective changes, views and vanishing points. Sicilian Baroque is noted above all for its colors, from the golden yellow of the tufa of Noto, to the white of Ragusa, the lava black of the buildings of Catania (with the volcano Etna nearby). The exuberance of the forms, the playfulness, the energy emanated by those colossal imposing sculptural and architectural monuments set with perspective precision into the streets and squares of the city is striking.

While Sicilian Baroque expresses itself above all in sacred buildings, but also in the palaces and residences built outside the city to escape the heat of summer and the traffic (so beautifully described in "The Leopard", with the spacious terraces of the Donnafugata villa overlooking sweeping panoramas).

Rosario Gagliardi is considered the most important architect

▶ Allegorical figures decorate Villa Palagonia in Bagheria.

of Sicilian Baroque. He is still relatively little known but succeeded in fusing elements of Sicilian folklore with the Baroque. He built in the hard-struck earthquake areas of Noto, Ragusa, Modica and in other lesser centers, concentrating on the exteriors, particularly the facades and spacious terraces. In his church architecture he inserted bell towers harking back to Byzantine times and the elements of splendor and elegance he added to the palaces and villas reflected the ranks of his powerful patrons. The *Church of San Giorgio in Ragusa* and the *Cathedral of Modica* are considered his masterpieces. Giovan Battista Vaccarini was a more cosmopolitan figure and was nominated architect prince of the city of Catania. He was particularly involved in town planning, above all the central Piazza del Duomo where he erected the *obelisk resting on an elephant*, clearly inspired by Bernini's Elephant Fountain in Rome. The third of the Sicilian Baroque artists was Giacomo Serpotta, who worked above all in church interiors where he fused tall spacious perspective views, the strength of marble with a sense of airy lightness, with touches of the neoclassic. He invented "grotesques" of Renaissance derivation, polychrome stuccoes, colored marble with the extravagance typical of Roman Baroque. His masterpiece is the *Oratory of the Rosary* in the *Church of Santa Cita in Palermo*.

◀▼ Stuccoes by Giacomo Serpotta in the Oratory of Santa Cita in Palermo and close-up of one of the decorated balconies of Villa Nicolaci in Noto.

NOTO

Much has been written regarding Noto, its unique typically Sicilian Baroque, the earthquake of 1693 that razed it to the ground and its rebirth, its honeycolored stone that glows like gold at sunset. Even so Noto seemed to have been forgotten until 1996 when the dome of the cathedral collapsed and the whole world was alarmed. The art historian Federico Zeri remarked "that bombs were needed to make Italy wake up". In the meanwhile in 1961 Michelangelo Antonioni chose it as setting for his film "The Adventure". Cesare Brandi defined Noto as the "ingenious garden-city of stone", and that is perhaps the best description of the city.

After the earthquake Noto was completely rebuilt in honey-colored tufa by the architects Rosario Gagliardi, Vincenzo Sinatra, Antonio Mazza, Paolo Labisi and Domenico Landolina, and with the fantasy of the master stone workers. Noto became a masterpiece-city, the unmistakable image and symbol of a southeastern Sicily of marvels. In June of 2002 the city, together with the towns in the Val di Noto, was declared a World Heritage Site by UNESCO. Since 2003 it also has a university.

The decision to rebuild Noto eight kilometers from old Noto was made by Giuseppe Lanza duke of Camastra, the representative of the Spanish viceroy, charged by the church and the land-owning nobles with rebuilding after the apocalyptic earthquake of 1693.

A few months later the construction of new Noto began, on the left of the Asinaro river, three kilometers from the sea, on the slopes of the Iblei mountains and overlooking the gulf.

The countryside around Noto consists of fields of wheat, olives and grapevines from which a sweet aromatic golden-yellow wine is made – the highly esteemed *Moscato di Noto*.

Aside from its noble buildings, wealth of churches and scenic settings, Noto is also a city full of pastry shops, sweet and chocolate shops, corners where the marvelous delicacies, from *torroni* to marzipan, from *cannoli* to jellies are put on show.

Noto is also striking for its marvelous eighteenth-century settings with sloping squares and streets, like *Corso Vittorio Emanuele* and the parallel *Via Cavour* with its superb palaces and churches and from which paved lanes and stairways seem to rise up perpendicularly. Strolling along these silent streets leads to unexpected and exciting discoveries. Entry to the city is by Corso Vittorio Emanuele, a kilometer long and cut by three piazzas: dell'Immacolata, del Municipio and XVI Maggio, from **Porta Reale** or **Ferdinandea**, built in 1838 in honor of Ferdinand II Bourbon (the sculptures of the tower, the pelican, the greyhound, symbols of strength, self-sacrifice and fidelity to

◄ A steep stepped street.

the Bourbons). There is a three tiered staircase overlooking the first piazza, at the top of which is the **Church of San Francesco dell'Immacolata** (former **Franciscan Convent**). On the left, the **Church** and **Monastery of San Salvatore** of 1706, with a pointed bell tower. Archaeological finds from the environs and the remains of ancient Noto are in the **Municipal Museum** inside the convent. The small **Church of Santa Chiara** opposite the monastery was built by Rosario Gagliardi in 1743. With a profusion of stuccos and gold, it contains a fine *Madonna and Child* by Antonello Gagini and an altarpiece with *Saint Scolastica and Saint Benedict* by the Palermitan artist Lo Forte. Masterpieces, such as the eighteenth-century

▼ ► Porta Reale or Ferdinandea and the Church of San Francesco dell'Immacolata.

▲▼ The Cathedral of Noto, before and after the collapse of the dome in 1996 and Palazzo Ducezio, seat of the town hall.

Cathedral dedicated to Saints Nicholas and Corrado, abound around the Piazza del Municipio, an elegant stage and rendezvous for the inhabitants.

The **Cathedral**, fenced off for restoration after the collapse of the dome, is flanked by twin bell towers and sits at the top of a monumental staircase with three landings. The facade is decorated with statues and bands of columns. To the right of the Cathedral is the nineteenth-century **Bishop's Palace** and, on the left, the **Palazzo Landolini** of the Marchesi di Sant'Alfano (an old noble Norman family) with two sphinxes in the courtyard. Facing the Cathedral is the rich **Palazzo Ducezio**, the town hall, built in 1746 by Vincenzo Sinatra. It has two stories and is surrounded on three sides by a colonnade. A splendid balcony is at the center of the facade on the convex part. Inside there is a *Hall of Mirrors* furnished in Louis XVI style. Not far off, along Corso Vittorio Emanuele, is the Church of San Carlo, followed by Piazza XVI Maggio with the **Theater**, the Dominican Church and Convent. The fine eighteenth-century **Church of San Carlo**

The **Sanctuary of San Calogero**, a popular pilgrim site, is six kilometers from the city. The 81 steps of the two storied bell tower can be climbed to get a fine panorama of the city, Portopalo and Capo Passero.

The superb **Dominican Church** and **Convent** are the monuments that best express the extraordinary Baroque of Noto. The entire complex is a masterpiece of elegance, by the architect Rosario Gagliardi with a facade that is convex in the central part and with a magnificent highly decorated portal.

Via Nicolaci is a perspective steep street, a crossing of Corso Vittorio Emanuele. At the top the backdrop is the **Church of Montevergini**; the famous **Palazzo Nicolaci**

al Corso or **del Collegio** with a nave and two aisles has two holy water stoups of Noto before the earthquake, and a rich eighteenth-century organ. To the right of the high altar is the Chapel of the patron saint of Noto, San Corrado Gonfalonieri, and in the Chapel on the left is the fifteenth-century chased silver *Reliquary* with the relics of the saint.

◀ ▼ The Church of San Domenico and the *Madonna of the Snows* by Francesco Laurana in the Church of the Crucifix.

▶ The Baroque balconies of Palazzo Nicolaci Villadorata.

Villadorata also faces the street with six balconies supported by allegorical figures projecting from the façade. The interior is just as rich with an immense *Ball Room*.

In the third week of May, Via Nicolaci is also the setting for the annual *Baroque Spring* of Noto, with the *Infiorata*, when the street is covered with artistic pictures made with a profusion of colored flower petals. Also to be seen is the fine statue of the *Madonna and Child*, or Madonna of the Snows by Laurana, in the **Church of Crocifisso**.

Ten kilometers from eighteenth-century Noto is Noto Antica, now covered with weeds and brushwood. All that is left of the old city are a **castle** and a **gymnasium** dating to the 3rd century B.C.

◀ ▼ The *infiorata* in Via Nicolaci.

SICILY AT TABLE

▲ The good bread of Sicily

▲▼ *Pasta con le sarde*,
a typical Sicilian dish and *peperonata*.

▲ *Arancini*, *panelle* and fried food.

While some of the Sicilian sweets and dishes could be thought of as typical of Sicily, such as *pasta con le sarde*, *pasta alla Norma* (Catania's homage to Vincenzo Bellini), or the *cassata* and the *cannoli*, you would be hard put to find a town that doesn't have a dish or sweet of its own for the holidays or Easter. In 330 B.C. the poet Archestratus of Gela extolled the Sicilian cuisine and cooks from here were often invited to Athens.

The tradition of Sicilian gastronomy is Mediterranean with bread and pasta, introduced by the Greeks, or the *focaccia* favored by the Romans. Bread in Sicily can be in any shape or size: long, round, oval, black or white, with sesame or cumin or fennel seeds, but it must be fresh (bakeries are open even on holidays). A Sicilian can't eat without bread. Pasta, dry or freshly home-made, reigns over the table, served with vegetables, tomato or ragù sauce, with the tasty oil and bread crumbs known as *cca muddica*, the Agrigento pesto made with pistachios, or the delicate ravioli filled with ricotta and mint or the fried pasta with oranges.

Rice was introduced by the Arabs and is used for timbales, sweets and the famous *arancini,* deep-fried rice balls with saffron and meat sauce and *caciocavallo* cheese. The Arabs also introduced couscous as well as spices and in the area of Trapani, together with fish, it is one of the main dishes to which a festival has been devoted.

The sun-ripened Mediterranean vegetables are bursting with flavor. Eggplants and bell peppers, celery, tomatoes and a variety of sweet zucchini almost thirty centimeters long are all used together in the ever-present *caponata*, and every city or town has its own version. The zucchini leaves, called *tenerumi*, are also cooked.

The puree of broad beans known as *maccu* made with chopped onions and tomatoes, or in salad, is exceptionally good. Pine nuts, almonds, walnuts, raisins and pistachios, here growing in abundance, accompany both main dishes and sweets. The typical meat in the Sicilian cuisine is kid or lamb. Fish, as is natural for an island, plays a large part in the diet: swordfish and tuna fish, oven-baked, smoked, fried, with tomato, or grilled, in grape leaves Greek-style, or seasoned with a good *salmoriglio* sauce. The *sarde a beccafico*, with bread crumbs, raisins and orange juice. And *sardines*, *squid*, *baccalà* and *stoccafisso* (dried cod) introduced by the men of the north.

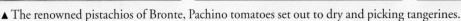

▲ The renowned pistachios of Bronte, Pachino tomatoes set out to dry and picking tangerines.

◀ Rounds of Madonie ricotta and the famous Sicilian cannoli.

▼ Marzipan sweets, quince delights and the *cassata*, a dessert that is the symbol of Sicily.

The French taught the use of the braised and gratineed onion and how to cover meat and certain vegetables with puff paste, like the *farsu magru*, rolls of meat filled with raisins, pine nuts, hard boiled eggs, cheese.

Oranges are added to salads with fennel, olives, tomatoes, as well as used in sweets. The *brasiliane* are excellent, large, not perfectly round, but succulent and sweet.

Sicily is the queen of sweets, with the *cassata*, the emir's sweet, a symbol of voluptuous food. The cassata was first created around 900 with the Arabs when a Saracen cook mixed ricotta and sugar in a copper tureen (hence the name *qas'at*), adding an apotheosis of candied fruit, sponge cake soaked in rum, and, with the Spanish, pieces of chocolate. The result is creamy with a delicate flavor and an intense aftertaste of fresh ricotta. The famous *cannoli*, like most of the Sicilian sweets, also use ricotta.

Frutta martorana known as the sweet with a celestial flavor – perhaps because it was created by the nuns in the convent la Martorana in Palermo – is prepared with almond paste and sugar and then colored. It is said that the nuns first made *frutta martorana* to decorate the trees in the garden for the visit of a bishop but that in 1575 this same bishop prohibited them from preparing sweets during Holy Week so they would not be distracted from their prayers. In some Sicilian households the Christmas tree is decorated with *frutta martorana*.

And then there are the granite, or ices, flavored with almonds, lemon, coffee, and ice cream introduced once again by the Arabs. A tradition of Trapani is the *scurzunera*, an ice prepared with jasmine buds, which are also used as an antidote against serpents (called *scursuni*). Delicious and delicate at the end of the meal are watermelon, melon and jasmine ices, dusted with cinnamon and pieces of chocolate.

◀▼ Decorating *frutta martorana* and the good Sicilian ice cream.

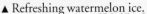

▲ Refreshing watermelon ice.

SYRACUSE (Siracusa)

"You shall tell the muses to remember Syracuse and Ortygia" are the words of the Greek poet Pindar, centuries after the Roman orator Cicero had defined it as "the most beautiful of Greek cities, and the most beautiful in the world" in his "*Verrine*". Syracuse is beautiful, enthralling, and timeless. The island of Ortygia floating on the water (one square kilometer), proud of its twenty-nine centuries of history and with its white stones, exuding and tasting of myth, is captivating. It has survived neglect and the onslaught of cement that has recently even taken over the old quarters of *Tyche, Acradina* and *Epipoli*, with its landscape defaced by the petrochemical industry, so far from what it used to be when it was a powerful Syracuse, Greek since 740 B.C., as imposing as Athens according to Plutarch and Thucydides. The immortal verses of Aeschylus, Sophocles, Euripides, Menander and Aristophanes are still recited in the splendid ancient Theater, center of the life and culture of Syracuse every year with the theater performances beginning at sunset, and the magical tragic ode resounding once more.

Ortygia, floating in the sea between the **Large Port** and the **Small Port**, embodies the soul of Syracuse. The city

▲▼ The harbor and the Jesuit Church and the seafront with the Maniace Castle.

has an intimate, indissoluble, relationship with the sea which made it rich and powerful. This glittering green sea appears everywhere between the *strigas* or lanes, the alleyways and narrow passageways, courtyards and vaults, and the odor of sea salt imbues every corner. When the sea is stormy the breakers wash over walls and doorways. The relentless scirocco also blows from the sea, and the lanes and alleys almost seem to serve as protection from

◀ ▲ Houses in Syracuse with the sea in the background and the fish market in Ortygia.

the biting air. With or without the scirocco, the Syracusans love to sit or walk, winter and summer, along the sea, the symbol of life: along the **Lungomare Alfeo**, or the **Passeggiata Aretusa** with its evocative **Fonte Aretusa**, the sweet water spring where papyrus plants grow and ducks splash about. Arethusa was the nymph in Ovid's story who abandoned Greece in her flight from the river god Alpheus who had fallen in love with her and was turned into a spring by the goddess Artemis. Alpheus however changed himself into an underground river and mingled his waters with those of his beloved. Everything in Syracuse has something mythical about it. Even its founding seems to have been foretold by the oracle of Delphi, a place dear to the Syracusans Theocritus and Epicharmus, and that genius of mathematics and philosopy Archimedes. It was thanks to the deadly war machines of Archimedes, who discovered the principle of floating bod-

▼ The mythical Fonte Arethusa where papyrus plants grow.

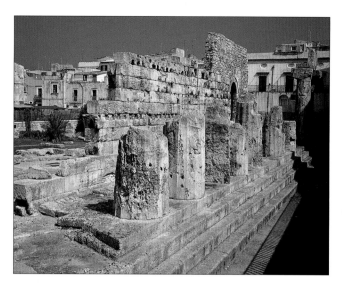

◄ The Doric Temple of Apollo.

"The Red Carnation" and above all in "Conversations in Sicily". The restaurants, cafes and coffee shops found everywhere serve the best almond flavored *granita* in Sicily, together with delicious dishes, especially fish.

Ortygia is gay, colorful and neat, an open-air museum, beginning with the Doric **Temple of Apollo**, the oldest, with its perpendicular little streets less than a meter wide, that start in **Piazza Archimede** and its Byzantine, Arab and balconied Baroque houses and palaces, mocking masks and geraniums everywhere. The semi-elliptical **Piazza del Duomo** is the highest point in Ortygia, once the site of the acropolis and now one of the evocative Baroque stages of the city overlooked by the **Palazzo Senatorio**, built by the Spanish architect Giovanni Vermexio and now the Town Hall, the **Palazzo Beneventano del Bosco** built by Luciano Alì, the **Bishop's Palace**, the **Church of Santa Lucia alla Badia** and finally the **Cathedral**. The Cathedral is an example of the stratification of Syracuse. In A.D. 640 the Byzantines incorporated the 5th century

ies, that Syracuse succeeded in holding out against the Romans for three years (215-212 B.C.) but the philosopher was then killed by a solider who paid no heed to the orders of the consul Marcellus who esteemed the scientist. The Fonte Aretusa also seduced another native son of Syracuse, the writer Elio Vittorini. Although he left his city to direct important publishing houses in the north of Italy, he devoted lovely pages to Syracuse in his novels

▼ Piazza del Duomo with Palazzo Senatorio, the Cathedral, the Bishop's Palace and Santa Lucia alla Badia.

B.C. temple of Athena built by the Greeks on an earlier 9th century temple of the Siculi. They turned it into a basilica and then it became a mosque and still later a Norman church. The opulent dynamic Baroque facade decorated with statues is an eighteenth-century reconstruction by the architect Andrea Palma. The Cathedral is a profusion of sculpture and painting. Outstanding on the high altar is a *ciborium* by Luigi Vanvitelli, and a sumptuous Baroque altar by Giovanni Vermexio flanked by fifteenth-century *choir stalls* in the sanctuary, while

▲▼ *Saint Zosimo*, panel attributed to Antonello da Messina and detail of the high altar in the Cathedral.

► The Baroque Cathedral of Syracuse.

by Antonello da Messina (1474) and the marvelous *Entombment of Saint Lucy* by Caravaggio.

The **Maniace Castle** on the point of Ortygia is a thirteenth-century castle built for Frederick II as his residence, on the site of the old temple of Juno, and where the Roman governor then lived. It has been greatly changed over the centuries and looks like a square fortress with massive cylindrical towers.

a twelfth-century *baptismal font* is in the first chapel in the right aisle. In the *Chapel of Saint Lucy*, patron saint of Syracuse, are a fine altarpiece and a silver statue of the saint (16th century). The people are profoundly devoted to Saint Lucy and celebrate her on the first Sunday in May as well as in December.

The nearby **Palazzo Bellomo**, the **Regional Museum**, has an interesting collection of nativity scenes, Arabian ceramics, medieval and Renaissance sculpture and paintings, including the splendid and famous *Annunciation*

The *polis* of Syracuse in the 5th century B.C. was at the height of its splendor and was divided into five great quarters, both urbanistically and administratively: *Ortygia, Acradina, Tyche, Epipoli* and *Neapolis*.

The archaeological zones where the white stone monuments that have made the city eternal are Acradina and Neapolis. In the old **Acradina**, where modern building needs were stronger than those of archaeology, one can still see the ruins of the **Syracusan Forum**, in a park, the **Roman Gymnasium**, with a theater that still has part

▼ ▶ *Annunciation* by Antonello da Messina and *The Entombment of Saint Lucy* by Caravaggio (Regional Museum of Palazzo Bellomo).

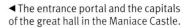
◄ The entrance portal and the capitals of the great hall in the Maniace Castle.

Persians" took place here and the spectators received gifts of perfumed unguents at the official opening. Dug into the rock of the Temenite hill, it faces the sea, with a cavea 138 meters in diameter and with 67 tiers subdivided into 9 sections. The altar dedicated to the god of intoxication and of wine, Dionysus, was in the **orchestra** between the stage and the cavea, with around it the chorus. The theater could seat twenty thousand spectators and was adapted by the Romans for gladiatorial games and simulated naval battles. A terrace dug into the rock overlooks the theater. There were also two **porticos** and the **grotto of the Nymphaeum**, a sacred site for religious ceremonies, with a vaulted ceiling and small votive niches dug into the walls and a basin. On the left is the **Via dei Sepolcri** (Street of the Tombs) with marks of cartwheel ruts and with small votive **niches** in the walls and Byzantine **hypogea**. In summer evenings the Theater of Syracuse is the setting for classic theater performances, a twenty-five century old tradition the *Istituto del Dramma Antico* has kept alive in Syracuse since 1914.

of the cavea and a few tiers, and the **Byzantine Baths**, now not much more than a pile of stones under an enormous apartment building. It is said that it was in one of the rooms of this building that a servant killed the emperor Constant II with a soup dish.

The fine **archaeological park of Neapolis** stretches over a wide area called **temenos** (sacred enclosure) by the Greeks. The **Theater** is the greatest monument of Greek theater architecture, built in the 5th century B.C. by Damacopos and modified by Hieron II in the 3rd century. The first performance of Aeschylus's tragedy "The

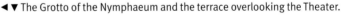
◄ ▼ The Grotto of the Nymphaeum and the terrace overlooking the Theater.

The **Latomie** (from the Greek *lithos* and *temno*, cut stone) are the quarries from which the white limestone for building the monuments was extracted in the 5th century B.C. They subsequently became prisons for the Greeks defeated in 413 B.C., who were forced to quarry the stone forty meters underground.

◄ ▼ Latomia of Paradise and the Ear of Dionysius.

Today the *latomie* are surrounded by splendid parks with citrus trees, oleanders, prickly pear and acanthus plants, and one has even been rechristened the **Latomia of Paradise**. Inside is the famous **Ear of Dionysius**, an artificial cavity 65 meters long and 23 meters high in the shape of a great ear. It supposedly received this name from Caravaggio in 1608. It is said the suspicious tyrant Dionysius listened to the complaints and laments of the prisoners thanks to the exceptional acoustics of the cave. The neighboring **Grotta dei Cordari**, where slaves once extracted rocks, was occupied by rope makers up to ten years ago. The so-called **Tomb of Archimedes**, in the form of a cave with a pediment, is in the **Necropolis of the Grotticelle**. All that is left of the imposing **Ara di Ierone**, the sacrificial altar erected by Hieron II in gratitude to Zeus, is the base which measures 198 by 23 meters. Two stairways decorated with atlas figures led to the altar where bulls were sacrificed. The historian Diodorus Siculus narrates that 450 bulls were sacrificed all on the same day and that the roast meat was then distributed to the city. The pool next to it dates to Roman times. The **Roman Amphitheater** where the circus games and the gladiatorial combats were held is an elliptical structure of the 3rd-4th century A.D. cut into the rock and surpassed in size only by the Colosseum and the Arena of Verona.

The remains of the **Euryalus Fortress** are in the old quarter of **Epipoli**, eight kilometers from the center. It is one of the finest example of Greek military architecture still extant and was built at the beginning of the 4th century B.C. by Dionysius the Elder on the highest point of the plateau overlooking the sea. The city had walls ten meters high and three wide, with three rings of ditches that made it possible to ward off enemy attacks. Five towers reinforced the **keep** and on one of them the catapults, formidable war machines designed by Archimedes, were set up. The Syracusans, always devoted to Mary, became even more so after the miraculous event of 1953 when an image of the Madonna began to shed tears. The city then built the **Shrine of Our Lady of Tears**, to which pilgrimages from all over the world arrive. It was built in 1966 and is seventy-four meters high and can be seen from all over the city. The painting of the *Madonna* is on the high altar inside. Near the Sanctuary is the old **Church of San Giovanni**, in the *Crypt* of which is the *tomb of Saint Marcian*, first bishop of Syracuse who became a martyr in the 3rd century A.D. under Valerian and Gallienus. The Catacombs were used by Christians during the Roman persecutions.

► The Shrine of Our Lady of Tears.

◀ *Sarcophagus of Adelfia and Valerio*, 3rd century A.D. (Paolo Orsi Museum).

▼ *Venus Anadyomene* known also as Landolina Venus (Paolo Orsi Museum).

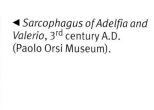

◀ *Enthroned goddess*, sixth century B.C. stele (Paolo Orsi Museum).

The rich **Paolo Orsi Archaeological Museum** is in the park of **Villa Landolina**. The 18,000 finds spread over an area of 9,000 sq. m. include skeletons of two dwarf elephants found in the grotto of Spinagallo, numerous amphoras and funeral furnishings. The bronze *kouros* found in nearby Lentini dates to the 6th century B.C.. The other one, with a dedication to the physician Sambrotidas on his leg, dates to 550 B.C. and comes from the excavations of Megara Hyblaea; a fine painted limestone sculpture representing the *Mother Goddess nursing twins* and the *Sarcophagus of Adelphia and Valerius* dating to the 3rd century A.D. Here is also the famous sculpture of *Venus Anadyomene* or *Landolina Venus* so-called after the man who discovered her. This is the fine Roman copy of a Greek original, maybe by Praxiteles. When he saw her, the French novelist Guy de Maupassant went into ecstasies because of her soft sensual body.

◀ ▲ *Mother Goddess nursing twins* and Greek *head* of the archaic period (Paolo Orsi Museum).

◀ The 3ʳᵈ century B.C. Greek theater in Palazzolo Acreide.

In the immediate vicinity of the city of Syracuse, towards the hinterland, there are any number of places with a wealth of history, art and things to see, to begin with the **Fonte Ciane**, a river supposed to have sprung from the tears of Cyane when her lady Persephone was forced to follow Hades into the underworld. Masses of flourishing papyrus plants grow on the banks of this charming site. The first papyrus plants were sent to Hieron II by Ptolemy II of Egypt and ever since Syracuse has made papyrus paper, and the city also has an interesting **Papyrus Museum**.

PALAZZOLO ACREIDE is the ancient *Akrai*, sub-colony of Syracuse founded in 664 B.C. Still remaining are the small 3ʳᵈ century B.C. **Greek theater** surrounded by carob trees, the **Bouleuterion** and the **Latomie dell'Intagliata** and **dell'Intagliatella**, ancient quarries used centuries later by Christians as dwellings and cemeteries. **PANTALICA** is in a gorge dug by the Anapo river, covered with vegetation and manna trees. The Hybla kingdom was here between the 13ᵗʰ and 8ᵗʰ century B.C. as attested to by the ruins of the **Anaktoron**, or prince's palace, at the tip of the valley overlooking the 5000 **burial chambers** dug into the rock walls that in the Middle Ages served as shelters for Byzantine hermits.

▼ ▶ The vast Necropolis and the remains of the Anaktoron in Pantalica.

▼ Manna tree and harvest.

PUPPETS AND CARTS, TRAGIC AND GAY HEART OF SICILY

▲ Angelo Grasso, a great actor on the Sicilian stage.

The Sicilian puppets, actually marionettes, are known as "*pupi*" and are of wood, moved by strings, and represent sumptuously dressed knights and ladies of times past, with veils, swords and suits of armor, who act out, in stentorian voices and with cries and moans, stories of love and death, charming the popular imagination from tiny, magic stages. The beginnings of the *Opera dei Pupi* go way back, perhaps to right after the Middle Ages when the great Romantic cycles of the paladins Orlando and Rinaldo and the beautiful Angelica enchanted the popular audiences of Europe. These stories found their way to Sicily in the nineteenth century where they reflected the tragic and exuberant nature of the Sicilian temperament. Battles, conflicts, loves, lives of saints and martyrs, brutal struggles to the death, thwarted passions – none other than the eternal struggle between good and evil – have always been what theater is about. In a setting both magical and realistic with glittering tin swords and suits of armature in an exotic eastern ambience, with kings, knights and lovely maidens, it has fascinated young and old.

The puppet theater exists almost everywhere in Sicily, but the original puppet theater must be seen in Palermo, its homeland, or in Catania where the *Teatro Stabile dell'Opera dei Pupi* has been established recently in the great complex of the Ciminiere, under the guidance of the Napoli family, puppeteers since 1921. The puppets of Catania can be distinguished from those of Palermo by their size. The former are larger, over a meter high, while those of Palermo are smaller and easier to move.

The magic created by these folk performances in the fragile puppet theaters spreads to the streets, above all for the feasts of the patron saints, the *sagras*, and other events with the appearance of the famous multicolored "Sicilian carts", true poignant joyous sculptures. The cart, today the colorful symbol of the island, was originally used for work, transporting grain,

◀▼ The characteristic marionettes of different sizes.

◀ Marionettes on stage.

▲▲ The typical cart and the Jew's harp, a Sicilian musical instrument.

stones and household goods. Then perhaps in imitation of the opulence carriages of the nobility, they were enriched and brightly painted. They gradually became true works of art, on which a variety of artisans worked – blacksmiths, decorators, carvers and painters. Every part of the cart was carefully done and painted in brilliant colors ranging from bright red to intense yellow to green, mostly in magical combinations, and varying depending on what part of Sicily they were in. Some carts are decorated with designs of fruits and plants, others have the fascinating stories of knights and ladies. If you can, go see some of the splendid collections of Sicilian carts, as in Modica, Palermo or Partico.

▼ Carnival in a cart.

▲▼ Decoration of a cart and a craftsman at work.

CATANIA

◄ ▲ ▼ The Feast of Saint Agatha, the *ripiddu 'nnivicatu*, a typical Catanian dish, and view of the city and of Etna.

Catania is the child of Etna, the imposing volcano that looms up over the city. In their eternal battle with that incandescent red river, when most afraid the Catanians bring out the *Santuzza Agata*, their patron saint who has saved the city before. The Catanians, volcanic like their mountain, represent another of Sicily's faces: ironic, rebel, shrewd, imaginative and enterprising, with a highly developed sense for business and trade to which the old local aristocracy has also converted. Catania is the second city in the island, in population and industry and first in income. The writer Guido Piovene has called it the Milan of the South. Between the volcano and the sea, between fire and water, in a plain of orange groves, the city was destroyed nine times and rose from its ashes nine times. It is the stronghold of the puppeteers and the puppet theater, the native land of great actors such as Giovanni Grasso and Angelo Musco, for whom Pirandello wrote the comedy "Pensaci Giacomino" (Think it over, Giacomino). Catania is an open city, and welcomes innovations, with room for all forms of cultural, musical and artistic experimentation. Musicians such as Vincenzo Bellini, writers such as Giovanni Verga, Federico De Roberto, Luigi Capuana, Vitaliano Brancati and the physicist Ettore Majorana were born here. This city that loves melodrama has dedicated a **Museum** to their "Catanian swan", Vincenzo Bellini, who wrote some of the most beautiful arias for female voices, as well as a **Theater** and even a recipe for "pasta alla Norma". A monument and public gardens bear his name. The house where Giovanni Verga was born, in Via Sant'Anna, is also a museum. Catania has been a university city since 1434. Alfonso of Aragon founded the first university **Sicolarum Gymnasium**, and it is attended by young people from all of Sicily.

▲ ▶ The gardens and the theater Catania dedicated to Bellini.

It is a fashionable city with fine shops, young people crowding the hundred and twenty pubs, discotheques, the twenty theaters and trendy rendezvous. When dusk falls, and the sea breeze arrives, it is time for the Catanian *movida* or promenade. The city is transformed into an open-air theater where staying up late is the rule. Eating well is also sacred and the traditional cuisine has branched out into imaginative versions such as the *arancini* with black squid ink and fish sauces. No one should leave Catania without tasting the *ripiddu 'nnivicatu* dedicated to their volcano: a dish of black squid ink rice with a flow of tomato sauce, dusted with ricotta. Even more mouth-watering is the Via Etnea, with cafes and pastry shops, such as the historical *Savia*.

The origins of Catania go back to the myth of Deucalion and Pyrrha, his wife, and the Cyclops who came down from Etna after a flood caused by Zeus. In Christian times the young martyr Agatha (251 A.D.) became the patron saint of the city. Every year from February 2 to 5, Catania dedicates a festival to their beloved *Santuzza*. Like other Sicilian cities, Catania was invaded by the Vandals, the Goths, and then three centuries of Byzantine domination followed by the Arabs, and then the Nor-

mans. The earthquake of 1169 destroyed Catania with fifteen thousand dead. Another calamity came in 1669 with the eruption of the volcano, one of the most terrifying in the memory of man, that left 6000 dead, while the victims of the earthquake of 1693 that swept away the city were sixteen thousand.

Catania today, Baroque and regal, in lava and in white limestone, of a Borrominian taste and elegance, with broad streets, palaces, convents and churches, was the fruit of the rebirth that took place in the decade beginning in 1694 during the reign of the Spanish viceroy. Of particular note among those involved were Giuseppe

Lanza duke of Camastra who designed the new city moving on horseback among the ruins and the young abbot-architect Giovanni Battista Vaccarini, the designer of the finest Catanian palaces in the historical center. *Piazza del Duomo* in Catania is the central square and soul of the city where the principal streets Via Etnea, Via Vittorio Emanuele and Via Garibaldi converge. The piazza is dominated by the monument that is the symbol of Catania, the celebrated **Elephant Fountain** in black basalt supporting an Egyptian obelisk with engravings to the goddess Isis on the side and with the emblem of Saint Agatha and a cross at the top. The fountain, which recalls the one by Bernini in Rome, was made by Vaccarini in 1736 and in its symbolism fuses pagan and Christian elements. The piazza, by the Palermitan architect Giovanni Battista Vaccarini, is surrounded by splendid Baroque palaces: the **Town Hall** in the former **Collegio dei Chierici** of 1741, then the **Porta Uzeda** of 1696 and lastly the **Cathedral**, dedicated to Saint Agatha

(there are eight other churches in Catania dedicated to this saint). Built by the Norman Roger in the 12th century it was practically destroyed in the earthquake of 1693. With the exception of three of its original apses, the transept and the flanking towers, all the rest is a reconstruction by Girolamo Palazzotto, while the opulent facade in two tiers with columns and the statue of the patron saint is by Vaccarini. Inside are the *sarcophagi of Vincenzo Bellini, Ferdinand of Aragon* and *queen Maria*. The remains of the Roman **Achillane Baths** are clearly visible. An elegant fifteenth-century portal by Giovan Battista Mazzolo leads into the **Chapel of the Madonna** with the *tomb of Constance of Aragon*. The **Chapel of Saint Agatha**, all pure gold and stuccoes, is in the right apse behind a wrought-iron gate. Traditionally, no one is allowed to enter with the exception of the priest and a few who have been the

▼ Piazza del Duomo, "heart of the city", with the Elephant Fountain, symbol of Catania.

to finish. The interior of the *Salone delle Feste* is particularly lavish, with mirrors, gilding, stuccoes and velvets and the **Galleria degli Uccelli** with a Neapolitan maiolica floor and fine Oriental porcelains. From the **terrace** with large windows and allegorical decorations there is a fine view of the sea. **Via Garibaldi** is the street opposite the cathedral, with the **Fountain of Amenano** (from the Amenano river underground) and the **Porta Carlo V** where the picturesque bustling **fish market** is held, winding through the lanes and alleys like a Near Eastern *suq*. Continuing along Via Garibaldi to Piazza Federico di Svevia one encounters the monumental **Ursino Castle**, seat of the **Municipal Museum**. The castle was built by Riccardo da Lentini for Frederick II between 1239 and 1250 for defense (control of the rebel city) and as a symbol of the affirmation of imperial power over the church. The seat of kings and parliaments, the rather austere ensemble has a large round tower at each corner. The rich **Municipal Museum** contains precious objects and donations from wealthy nobles and collectors in Catania. In the archaeological section, in addition to Greek black and red-figure vases from the *Biscari collection*, there are fragments of the Roman amphitheater, columns, obelisks, and a splendid *head of an ephebus* of the 6th century B.C. There is also a *Last Judgement* by Fra Angelico, a *Saint John the Baptist* by Pietro Novelli and a lovely *Madonna and Child* (1497) by Antonello de Saliba.

recipients of miracles. The altar is completely taken up by a fifteenth-century marble triptych by Antonello Freri depicting *Saint Agatha crowned by Jesus*. The relics of the saint, the famous veil – said to have stopped the flow of lava in 1669 – and the objects used for the feast of the Saint and carried in procession in the *cannalore*, processions with great painted wooden candles carried on the shoulders, are in the **Treasury**. There is also a fourteenth-century silver bust of the saint holding her skull, and the crown of diamonds and precious stones given by Richard the Lionheart to his sister Joan when she married William II. Worthy of note also are the **Chapel of the Sacrament** and the fifteenth-century wooden *choir stalls*, with rich intarsias with episodes from the life of the patron saint. A fresco in the **sacristy** depicts the *Eruption of Etna* in 1669.

Behind the Cathedral is **Palazzo Biscari**, one of the most opulent Baroque residences in Catania, which belonged to Prince Paternò Castelli. It was begun in the 18th century and what with additions and changes took a hundred years

► Ursino Castle, built for Frederick II, seat of the Municipal Museum.

tron saint are kept and the **House** and **Museum of Bellini**. The first of the five churches on Via Crociferi, after the Arch of San Benedetto, is that of **San Benedetto** with annexed the **Convent of the Poor Clares**, built in 1713, at the top of a staircase. A double ramp of stairs leads to the **Church of San Francesco Borgia**, built by the architect Angelo Italia. Opposite is the **Church** and former **College of the Jesuits**. The splendid **Church of San Giuliano** by Vaccarini of 1760 has a convex facade and a gallery around it, with a dome. In the elegant **Piazza Dante** at the end of Via Crociferi is the **Church of San Nicolò**, built in 1687 by the architect Contini but never finished. It is the largest religious building in Sicily, forty-eight meters wide and fifty-five long. The walls of the nave and side aisles are

Via Vittorio Emanuele is parallel to Via Garibaldi and is lined with churches, convents and Baroque palaces, such as the exclusive **Collegio Cutelli**, to which the aristocracy sent their children, and the **Badia Sant'Agata**, a monumental church with a chiaroscuro play of forms on the facade and a large octagonal dome. Once more built by Vaccarini in 1742, it is considered his masterpiece. On the same street is the entrance to the **Roman Theater** and the small semicircular **odeon**, of Greek origin, reused by the Romans (2nd-3rd century A.D.).

"Short, but infinitely beautiful" is how Vitaliano Brancati defined **Via Crociferi**, Catania's most monumental and distinctive street with a wealth of Baroque buildings. It begins at **Piazza San Francesco** with the **Church of San Francesco** where the *candelore* for the feast of the pa-

▼ ► The Monastery of San Nicolò, now university premises, and the scenic courtyard of the *Sicolarum Gymnasium*.

decorated with seventeenth-nineteenth-century paintings. There is a fine sundial in the transept, and twenty four slabs in the floor are marked with the *signs of the zodiac*. The **Church of Sant'Agata al Santo Carcere** is in a fine Gothic style and contains the cell where Saint Agatha was imprisoned and where she was martyred. **Via Etnea**, along the road leading up from Piazza del Duomo to Etna, once a street of the bourgeoisie and today, of exclusive shops, runs through *Piazza dell'Università*, with the premises of the Siculorum Gymnasium laid out around a scenographic courtyard, and *Piazza Stesicoro*, dedicated to the Greek 6th century B.C. poet, where the ruins of the **Roman amphitheater** are to be found (2nd century B.C.).

There are delightful places in the hinterland and along the coast in the environs of Catania, such as: **ACI CASTELLO** where the Catanians love to go swimming at the foot of the Byzantine black lava **Castle** that houses a **Municipal Museum**.

ACI TREZZA is the neighboring small fishing town celebrated by Giovanni Verga in his novel "*I Malavoglia*" (The House by the Medlar Tree). Luchino Visconti set his film "The Earth Trembles" here. Acitrezza is today a delightful seaside resort. The imposing black *Faraglioni dei Ciclopi* or Rocks of the Cyclops keep watch over the coast.

The Romans turned **ACIREALE**, a town on citrus tree terraces overlooking the sea, into a rich spa center. The **Terme di Santa Vènera** are still operating and together with the carnival celebrations attract hosts of tourists. Acireale also has a **Cathedral** with a picturesque facade with neo-Gothic elements, flanked by two bell towers with majolica spires.

◄ ▼ The facade of the Cathedral of Acireale and the *Fercolo (litter) of Saint Sebastian*, patron saint of the city.

THE WRATH OF THE GOOD GIANT

The mountain rose from the sea 500,000 years ago, is 3,340 meters high, 60 kilometers in diameter and has a perimeter of 212 kilometers. There are 250 erupting cones and 2 craters (the one at the top is an enormous funnel with a circumference of 3 kilometers). Rivers of incandescent lava flow out at a temperature of 1200° C and moving at a speed of 15 kilometers. This is Etna, the largest volcano in Europe, one of the most active in the world, relatively young and never still.

The Sicilians call this fascinating volcano *Mongibello* (*Mons Gebel* in Arabic) or *a muntagna*. This mystical mountain dominates the entire coast of eastern Sicily and its snow-capped cone can also be seen from the center of the island. The history of this corner of Sicily is marked by its eruptions, mentioned as early as 475 B.C. by Pindar and Aeschylus. One of the most cataclysmic was the eruption of 1669 that wiped out four towns and left six thousand dead in Catania. When fear strikes the hearts of the inhabitants, they put their trust, with processions and prayer, in the miraculous intervention of the many saints that people the towns on its slopes: Saint Agatha, Saint Egidio, Saint Anthony and the Madonna. But they know that *a muntagna pigghia, a muntagna dugna* (the mountain takes and the mountain gives), and the flourishing nature, fertile soil, the equivalent of gold for agriculture, are gifts from the mountain. After it has wreaked its fury, everything will be rebuilt. Olive and citrus groves, vineyards, almond and pistachio trees grow on the clods of soft black earth at the base of the volcano while further up the Mediterranean maquis flourishes and still further up there are splendid woods of beech, pine, cedars of Lebanon, birch, chestnut, and then pastures. At the very top at two thousand meters one comes to the extra-

ordinary lunar landscape, a stone garden, with reddish sponge-like rocks covered with snow in winter. In spring when the snows melt, what remains is a black desert where life seems impossible and yet cushions of milk vetch grow here, brightly colored meadows of soapwort, the symbol of Etna, and many other native species in unlikely colors. To safeguard the flora and fauna the Sicilian Region has instituted the Natural Park of Etna, where fascinating outings can be made and with many shelters where one can rest.

TAORMINA

▲▼ The Badiazza with snow-capped Mount Etna in the background, and bird's-eye view of Taormina suspended over the sea.

A mazement is what fills the visitor when he arrives in Taormina, an enchanted place, a city where one seems to be living in another world.

Taormina is the most aristocratic, most celebrated gem of tourist Sicily, with centuries of history, blessed by Mother Nature. Even the most demanding plants blossom in its microclimate. Goethe loved it and for Guy de Maupassant the landscape had everything created on earth to seduce the mind, the eye, and the fantasy of men. It has always seduced nobles, intellectuals, rulers, photographers, writers, statesmen and some of the first Grand Tour travelers who discovered it. Many settled there and since 1863 Taormina has been the capital of international elite tourism. Before then it had charmed Greeks and Romans. For the poet Ovid who celebrated its refined cuisine it was paradise. D.H. Lawrence, the English writer who fell in love with this land, lived there for three years in the 1920s and for many years Piazza IX Aprile bore witness to the love and drinking parties of Richard Burton and Liz Taylor.

Taormina is in an unbelievably fabulous position, on a rocky terrace on a promontory of Mount Tauro (from here the ancient name of *Tauromenion*). It is suspended two hundred meters above the Ionian sea, facing the coasts of Calabria and with Etna looming up on high. Bays, coves and beaches of rock, sand and gravel, Capo Taormina, Mazzarò, Isolabella and Capo Sant'Andrea, embrace it down below. The *beach of Mazzarò* is the most elite beach, while the *Baia di Isolabella* is an islet clothed in green with a castle and connected to the shore by a tongue of sand and now a WWF reserve. **Capo Sant'Andrea** is a fragrant oasis of Mediterranean maquis and a blue Grotto for swimming. Imposing *faraglioni* dominate the *Baia delle Sirene* at *Capo Taormina*.

The city promotes countless cultural events in its splendid Greek theater: the *Taormina Film Festival*, the *Festival Taormina Arte*, plays and fashion shows. With luxurious and splendid hotels, health spas, restaurants, cafes, exclusive shops it offers everything needed for light-hearted living and recreation of the body. Taormina of course also has its history and monuments. It has been Greek at heart since the 8th century B.C. when the Chalcidean Theokles shipwrecked on the coast and fell in love with the site and founded *Taumerion*. Occupied in 358 B.C. by the tyrant Dionysius of Syracuse, then the Greek Andromachus (father of the historian Timeon) repopulated it with survivors from the neighboring Naxos, and a new Greek city blossomed. It became Roman and then, with Augustus, was repopulated by Roman citizens after

▲ The evocative 3rd century A.D. Greek Theater of Taormina, facing the sea.

the original inhabitants who had supported Sextus Pompeius were sent into exile. Then came the Byzantines, the Vandals and the Arabs. Taormina was the last city they conquered, on August 1, 902 after a century of violent sieges. Afterwards came the Normans and Frederick II, struck by its tranquillity and silence, raised it to the imperial dignity. The Aragonese built the splendid palaces. Taormina's renaissance began with the Grand Tour but it was the photographs of the German photographer Wilhelm von Gloeden that finally brought Taormina worldwide fame. Taormina still has its ancient urban layout, with narrow steep streets, small squares and courtyards full of flowers, above all colorful bougainvilleas. The best way to see Taormina is on foot, climbing up the flower-filled staircases or going to the top by cable car.

The elegant **Corso Umberto I** stretches from **Porta Messina** to **Porta Catania**. It is the promenade of Taormina, the old Roman consular road *Valeria*, that joined Messina to Catania, while

the most important monument and symbol of Taormina, the **Greek Theater**, second largest in Sicily, after that of Syracuse, is on *Piazza Vittorio Emanuele*. Hugging the flank of Mount Tauro and facing the sea, it provides a fascinating panorama of the coastline, the Giardini Naxos and Etna. A hemicycle with a **cavea** a hundred and nine meters in diameter and surrounded by a double vaulted **portico**, the theater was built in the 3rd century B.C. and restored by the Romans. The **tiers** are divided into nine sectors and the **stage** (*scena*) with passageways flanked by

► The so-called Naumachia, a retaining structure dating to imperial times.

▲ ► The Church of Sant'Agostino in Piazza IX Aprile and Palazzo dei Duchi di Santo Stefano.

niches and columns opened onto the **orchestra**, used by the Romans for gladiatorial games. There was room for five thousand spectators. An **Antiquarium** has been set up at the entrance to the theater. The **Church of Santa Caterina** nearby was built in the late seventeenth century on the ruins of the old Roman **odeon**, incorporating some of the parts. Facing it is the **Palazzo Corvaja**, seat in 1411 of the first Sicilian parliament. The facade is a lacework of elegant two-light windows and a fine Gothic-Catalan portal. It now contains the **Museo delle Arti e Tradizioni Popolari** (folklore museum), and the tourist offices. All that remains of the Roman **Naumachia** are a hundred and twenty meters of wall marked by eighteen niches, a wall for what was once an enormous cistern. The scenic **Piazza IX Aprile**, with the Baroque **Fountain** and the **Clock Tower** is a panoramic lookout over the bay of Taormina and Etna, crowded with open-air cafes and pastry shops. The **Churches of Sant'Agostino** and **San Giuseppe** face out onto the square. The entrance to the old hamlet of Taormina with its lanes and alleys offering glimpses of the sea comes

after the Clock Tower. The 13th century **Cathedral** was renovated in the course of the centuries and is dedicated to San Nicolò. The austere facade has a fine rose

► The austere 13th century Cathedral of San Nicolò.

▶ The popular beach of Giardini Naxos.

window, and there is a polyptych with a *Madonna and Child* by Antonello de Saliba in the three-aisled interior.

GIARDINI NAXOS, the first Greek colony in Greece according to Thucydides, is now a splendid and popular seaside resort on the beach between Capo Taormina and Capo Schisò. Of interest are the **Excavations of Naxos** with traces of the ancient walls, buildings, dwellings, and the ruins of a temple dedicated to Aphrodite of the 6th and 5th century B.C. There is a collection of vases, amphoras, terracottas and anchors, and finds from the bottom of the sea in the **Archaeological Museum**. Fourteen kilometers of road lead from Giardini Naxos to Randazzo and the spectacular *Gole dell'Alcantara*, deep ravines and gorges in the basalt, with at the bottom the Alcantara river fed by a spring in the Nèbrodi mountains. The site is fascinating and today there are only frogs in the river (wear rubber boots to walk along it), but the Arabs raised crocodiles in the *al-Qantarah*.

▼ ▶ The Park of the Nebrodi and the spectacular Gole dell'Alcantara.

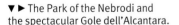

ANTONELLO, COMET OF MESSINA

Antonello da Messina passes through the story of world art like a splendid comet. He was born around 1430 and died in 1480. Little is known of the life of this enigmatic artist. For an idea of who Antonello da Messina was we must turn to Vasari's "romanticized" version of his life (in his "*Lives*" of the artists), and whatever bits of information he had available.

Antonello, the son of a marble master, was apprenticed to Colantonio (in Naples), personally knew Jan Van Eyck or was influenced by the painting of this Flemish artist (thus learning the technique of oil painting). He went to Rome and Venice (where he possibly influenced the golden era of Venetian fifteenth-century art, of the Bellinis and the Vivarinis), then to Florence where he was in turn influenced by Piero della Francesca and his use of perspective. Lastly he went to Milan but was not happy there and returned home to Messina.

Antonello is the greatest fifteenth-century south Italian painter (his work was continued by a certain Matteo Costanzo). He was an innovator and experimented with new pictorial techniques ranging from perspective to an interest in details to luminous colors, in pictures that revealed the inner soul of the sitter.

With his masterpieces Antonello renewed the genre of portrait painting, no longer ideal, no longer in profile, but three-quarter. He is the first truly modern portrait painter, precursor of that realism of which Caravaggio, two centuries later, was to be the great master. According to Antonello "the face is the only and sole real protagonist of the portrait picture, the rest is something added on".

▲◄ Detail of the *Polyptych of Saint Gregory* and *Self-portrait*.

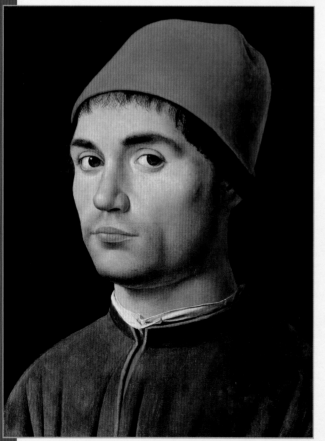

He was meticulous in his attention to surface verity, to the physiognomy and the subtle characteristics of his subjects, whom he steeped in an intense light, the main element in portraiture, with an almost photographic spotlighting of their features.

Among his most important works: the *Polyptych of Saint Gregory* (Messina), the famous *Annunciation* with an eastern influence, and a search for form and detail that make it unique (Palazzo Bellomo in Syracuse); the splendid portraits in Cefalù (his *Self-portrait* with five o'clock shadow and the features of a common man), the famous *Virgin of the Annunciation* (considered his greatest masterpiece) in Palermo in the Abatellis Museum. All together his work has a mysterious and explosive vitality, humanity, a familiarity, with a certain something in the eyes, the enigmatic smile, that recalls Leonardo da Vinci, almost imperceptibly veiled by a subtle orientalizing taste and that explosion of light that accentuates the figure, the virginal beauty of the woman-child, the brilliant precious blue.

The place of Antonello da Messina in the history of art is unique and of prime importance for Venetian art and the Bellinis who ideally continued the grace and pictorial tenderness of the master from Messina.

▲ ▶ The *Virgin Annunciate* and *Portrait of an Unknown Man*.

▲ The sublime *Annunciation* with orientalizing influences.

MESSINA

There is something surreal about arriving in Messina early in the morning or at sunset, when light floods the coast, for the city itself is hidden in fog, mists and haze. As they gradually dissolve the *Madonna della Lettera* in the port welcomes the traveler. The statue so dear to the inhabitants of Messina stands on a long shaft, and at the base of the votive column is an inscription that reads "We bless you and your city", words connected to a story or legend that lies at the origins of her worship. In far-distant 42 A.D. the Madonna is said to have sent a letter to the city together with a lock of hair and the phrase on the stele. For centuries the letter was kept in the city's Cathedral until it was destroyed in the fire of 1253.

Geographically Messina is considered the center of the Mediterranean sea in a splendid location between the Peloritani mountains, the peninsula of San Raineri and the sea.

▼ ▶ The "Madonna della Lettera" keeps watch over the deep straits, populated by swordfish.

The harbor is a broad natural sickle-shaped bay recalling that of Trapani. The Greeks who founded it in the 8th century B.C. called it *Zancle*, or sickle.

The history of Messina with its harbor and straits is one calamity and earthquake after the other. Beginning with antiquity, the source of its fame and wealth was the harbor. For centuries it was the port for the merchants of Amalfi, Florence, Venice and the East. Messina was the port of call for the international trade in spices, textiles and silks. Many of the activities related to the harbor, the deepest in Sicily, are still at the basis of its economy, for in addition to cruise ships, it is used by military ships of Italy and NATO and the ferries that

daily connect Sicily to Calabria. The straits are its fortune and at the same time an atavistic burden. The cobalt sea is dangerous, with counter-currents that collide, forming whirlpools. The descending current moves from the Tyrrhenian to the Ionian, and the rising one from the Ionian to the Tyrrhenian. They change direction every six hours so that the two seas have contrasting phases in their tides. These eddies and whirlpools lie at the basis of the legend of Scylla and Charybdis, Scylla on this side and Charybdis on the Calabrian side. These horrendous monsters pulled ships sailing through the waters of the strait down into the depths of the sea. From May to September the swordfish arrive in shoals in the strait to breed, and the sea of Messina every year is the stage for adventurous deep-sea fishing on special boats, known as *feluche*, where songs, cries and prayer accompany these age-old techniques. *U pisci spadu* is the prince of the table in Messina and is prepared in various ways: in the saucepan with oranges, sauce, raisins, or grilled. Swordfish sliced thin and smoked is also delicious.

Three kilometers separate Messina from the continent, from Calabria, and a plan to build a bridge or tunnel joining the two shores has been in the offing for forty years. A special association for the straits has been created but the problems connected with this gigantic project are many, both political and economic. The troubled history of Messina is marked by recurrent epidemics of the plague and cholera, earthquakes and seaquakes. The two most disastrous were in 1783 and 1908, destroying the city completely, with over eighty thousand dead in the latter. In World War II Messina was bombed more than any other city in Italy. What little remains of the old city has been incorporated into aseismic buildings and today Messina is a modern city, with broad tree-shaded avenues and low white reinforced concrete houses.

Messina is the port of Sicily, a city of passage and therefore not particularly Sicilian in spirit. But more continental, more tending to contacts and commerce outside the island, and economically more closely bound to the cities of the continent than those of the island.

The remains of fifteenth-century defensive fortifications against the Turks and the *Column of the Madonna* are on the **Raineri peninsula**, which closes the harbor on the east and marks the entrance to the city. The most im-

portant arteries are *Via I Settembre*, leading to the center from the sea, and *Via Garibaldi*, parallel to the port, while **Piazza del Duomo** with its Cathedral dedicated to the Our Lady of the Assumption is the heart of Messina. The most significant building in the city is the **Cathedral**, originally Norman and now rebuilt. It still has the lower part of the original facade with three Gothic portals. The largest one in the center is marked by a pair of lions supporting twisted columns, a statue of *Our Lady*, cherubs, kings and saints. The only original works inside are the fifteenth-century *Saint John the Baptist* by Antonello Gagini and the *tombstone of Bishop Palmieri* of 1195. The Cathedral **Treasury** has a magnificent *Golden Mantle* of 1668, a veil embroidered with precious stones and used in Orthodox rites. Next to the Cathedral is a bell tower sixty meters high, with a mechanical astronomical clock inside that comes to life at noon with signs of the zodiac and various tableaux appearing every fifteen minutes. The clock is the

► The astronomical clock of the 1930s on the bell tower next to the Cathedral.

▼ ► The Cathedral of Messina flanked by its tall bell tower and view of the nave.

largest in the world and was made in the 1930s in Strasbourg by the Ungerer brothers.

The fifteenth-century **Fountain of Orion** opposite the Cathedral is by Giovanni Angelo Montorsoli and Domenico Vanello and miraculously came through the earthquakes unscathed. The statues decorating the fountain represent the four rivers: Tiber, Ebro, Nile and Camaro. The **Santissima Annunziata dei Catalani** is a delightful Norman *pieve* or country parish church of the 12th century, with Arab influences. The earthquake destroyed all later additions. The fifteenth-century *Monument to John of Austria*, victor of the battle of Lepanto in 1571 against the Turks, is at the center of Piazza Catalani, opposite the church.

The rich **Regional Museum** contains fourteenth-century Byzantine and Sicilian paintings, sculpture and mosaics, panels with the *story of the letter of the Madonna*. A fine *majolica tondo* is from the workshop of Andrea della Robbia. Some of the exceptional masterpieces in the **Picture Gallery** include the *Adoration of the Shepherds* and the *Resurrection of Lazarus* by Caravaggio, who lived in Messina between 1608 and 1609. Of the great Antonello, a native of Messina, are the famous *Saint Gregory polyptych*, five oil panels and a small panel repre-

senting a *Madonna and Child and a monk* and, on the reverse side, *Christ crowned with thorns*. There is also a *Madonna and Child* by Antonello de Saliba and a lovely *Madonna and Child* by Laurana.

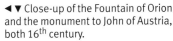

◀ ▼ Close-up of the Fountain of Orion and the monument to John of Austria, both 16th century.

▲ The imposing Milazzo Castle,
built by Frederick II on the ruins of the Acropolis.

Tindari with its Hellenistic and Roman ruins is splendidly located on a hill overlooking the gulf of Patti and its famous romantic small rock pools known as *Laghetti di Marinello*.

The Greek **Theater** is truly splendid, white and set against the side of a hill facing the sea. This hemicycle sixty-three meters in diameter was built at the end of the 4th century B.C. and was remodeled in

▼ The romantic pools of Marinello and the remains of a Roman house in Tindari.

Torre Faro, Ganzirri, Mortelle, are the beaches of the Messinesi, in the midst of verdant landscapes, rocky crags rising sheer from the sea and beaches of fine sand on a transparent green-blue sea. Splendid landscapes like these can be found along most of the Tyrrhenian coast, as at **MILAZZO** the ancient Greek *Mylai* founded in 716 B.C. and dominated by the old **Castle** built by Frederick II on the remains of the ancient Acropolis. Milazzo still has its medieval historical center, the old Cathedral and the **Church of the Rosary** with the Dominican convent, once headquarters of the *Inquisition*, and the **Basilica of San Francesco di Paola**. Capo Milazzo has splendid beaches with natural pools in the rocks, the **Shrine of Saint Anthony of Padua** with old ex-votos, and the **Grotta di Polifemo** where Ulysses is said to have encountered the Cyclops.

The gem of the Tyrrhenian coast near Messina is **TINDARI**, whose praises were sung by the Sicilian poet and Nobel Prize Salvatore Quasimodo *"I know you mild between broad hills, overhanging the waters of the god's sweet islands. Today, you confront me and break my heart"*...

▲ The splendid white Greek Theater of Tindari overlooking the sea.

Roman times. The entrance gate and a few towers are all that remain of the old fortified **walls** that surrounded the city while remains of shops, dwellings and the small 3rd century B.C. **baths** with mosaic pavements bear witness to the **insula** or city block on terraces moving towards the sea. In the *frigidarium* of one of the baths is a scene of wrestling athletes signed by *Agathon slave of Dionigi*. A ground floor room with barrel vaulting is all that is left of the three-story **Roman basilica** or **gymnasium**. Restoration using modern materials has not improved the structure. The **Archaeological Museum** contains finds from the excavations, including a fine stone *head of Augustus*.

Many come to Tindari to see the archaeological site, but the modern **Sanctuary of the Madonna of Tindari** also attracts many visitors. Pilgrimages have been coming to worship this *icon of the black Virgin* since Byzantine times. Her feast day now is September 8.

Not far from Tindari is the medieval town of **CAPO D'ORLANDO** at the base of the Rupe del Semaforo promontory. It was named – according to the inhabitants, but it may be legend – for one of Charlemagne's officers who built the **castle** of which the ruins are still visible. Next to it is the fifteenth-century **Shrine of Santa Maria Santissima** with a fine *Madonna of the Assumption* that is taken in procession on the fishing boats on August 15. Capo d'Orlando is a popular seaside resort with sinuous recesses and coves with sandy beaches such as Testa di Monaco and di Roccia, and that of San Gregorio with its charming lake.

▶ A stretch of the Costa San Gregorio at Capo d'Orlando.

EOLIE or LIPARI ISLANDS

Seven volcanic cones offshore Milazzo form the Aeolian archipelago, dream islands surrounded by a crystal-clear sea. Alicudi, Filicudi, Lipari, Panarea, Salina, Stromboli and Vulcano are where tourists go to get the best of what Sicily has to offer: sun, sea, a good climate, magical landscapes, flourishing vegetation, spa waters, swimming in water with a wealth of aquatic flora including red gorgonians, meadows of poseidonia oceanica and starfish, an excellent cuisine, entertainment, relaxation and silence. These islands are volcanic outcrops that emerged from the sea a million years ago. Two of them, Vulcano and Stromboli, are still active. Recently another underwater volcano has been discovered two kilometers from the latter, at a depth of five hundred meters. Fertile and with birds of all kinds as well as playful dolphins, they have been declared a World Heritage Site by UNESCO.

VULCANO, named by the Romans in honor of the god Vulcan, smells of sulphur. The smallest of the four small volcanoes that make up the island is Vulcanello and the largest and most active is Vulcano della Fossa. It is known for the therapeutic properties of its sulphurous mud and fumaroles or jets of steam and sulphur vapors rising from the clefts in the *faraglioni di Levante*. There is a haunting beauty to the island with its sulphur yellow and alum white rocks. The beaches include the *Spiaggia dell'Acqua Calda*, with hot water throughout the year,

◀ ▼ The Spiaggia dell'Acqua Calda at Vulcano and a spectacular view of rocks and craters colored yellow by the sulphur.

▲▲ The square white houses so typical of Stromboli.

that of *Ponente* or of the black sands with cane brakes (the women use the canes for making baskets and the men for their fishpots), and the semi-deserted *Gelso* with its lighthouse, all within walking distance.

STROMBOLI. After seventeen years of lull, in 2002 this volcano began erupting, resulting in a seaquake when two landslides took place in the wake of the fiery volcanic lava flow. The volcano is an important drawing card for the many tourists who climb up four hundred meters to enjoy the spectacle. It is also fascinating at night from the sea when the volcanoes shoot incandescent stones high into the sky. The Romans thought of it as the lighthouse of the Mediterranean. **Ginostra** and **Stromboli**, **San Vincenzo** and **Ficogrande** are the hamlets on the island of Stromboli, a few square white houses nestled in a flourishing vegetation of olives, vines, with bougainvillea on the walls. The population numbers fewer than a thousand, and donkeys are used for transportation. Stromboli, the

island favored by intellectuals and thinkers, in 1949 witnessed the love story between Roberto Rossellini and Ingrid Bergman during the shooting of the film "*Stromboli*".

SALINA, the old Greek *Didyme*, second largest in the archipelago, is the greenest of the Aeolian islands with vines, capers, fragrant broom. Salina (named after the old saltpans at the small town of Lingua) is dominated by two inactive volcanic cones and is in vogue for those who want beauty without noise and confusion. The lovely Mount Fossa delle Felci and the splendid amphitheater shaped lava beach of *Pollara* provide unforgettable sunsets. The beach became famous with Massimo Troisi's last film "*Il Postino*" with Maria Grazia Cucinotta. The cuisine of Salina offers any number of dishes based on capers, grown here since antiquity. When they blossom the fragrance of these white evanescent caper flowers inundate the island. One in particular of the excellent local wines, Malvasia, a muscatel, is the best in Sicily.

◀▼ Lava rocks on the sea of Pollara and the hamlet of Salina.

▲ The small and exclusive island of Panarea.

PANAREA is barely three square kilometers in size, the smallest of the islands, but the bluffs are exclusive and fashionable, the center of night life and riotous fun. The six surrounding cliffs can be reached on the small double ended fishing boats in the small harbor. Many Italians from the north have bought splendid white houses in the island's three districts: **Ditella**, **San Pietro** and **Drauto** (after the pirate Dragut). At the charming **Capo Milazzese** the ruins of the prehistoric village overlook the splendid bay of *Cala Junco* between two cliffs and the emerald sea. *Spiaggia Fumarola* is an isolated place with a pebbly beach where one can go swimming in absolute peace accompanied by the cries of the seagulls.

ALICUDI is covered with purple heather and prickly pear. It is the island of silence, mysterious and distant, without roads, only mule paths and donkeys. The few vacation houses are those the fishermen make available for those who want a vacation of sun and sea.

FILICUDI like Alicudi is wild, full of volcanic craters. The rocky coasts rise sheer from the sea but in some stretches, such as **Capo Graziano**, they are a bit friendlier. A *prehistoric village*, older than the one in Panarea, has

◄ ▼ Silent Alicudi and the prehistoric village of Capo Graziano at Filicudi.

◄ ▲ Marina Corta at Lipari and theater masks in the Archaeological Museum.

been discovered here. The pebbly beach *Pecorini a Mare* is right below the village. The *Grotta del Bue* is a cavern colored yellow, pink, green and azure, due to the volcanic gases.

LIPARI, the largest and most densely populated of the Aeolian Isles, is a black and white island: white with pumice and black with obsidian. It has tourist facilities and five small towns: **Canneto**, **Acquacalda**, **Quattropani**, **Piano Conte** and **Lipari**.

The principal town is Lipari, with splendid square houses colored pink, yellow, green, Pompeiian red, crowded together. There are cafes, hotels and restaurants.

Lipari is the island which appeared to Homer's Ulysses as an enchanted land. **Monte Pilato** with its white pumice

and **Rocche Rosse** black with obsidian are magical, dropping sheer to the sea, with spectacular color contrasts. The most famous beach, with a white pumice sand, is in the town of **Canneto**. The panorama of the island, the sea, the *faraglioni* and Vulcano from the *lookout point of Quattrocchi* is spectacular.

The interesting **Museo Archeologico Eoliano** (Aeolian Archaeological Museum) in the Spanish castle has prehistoric finds, sculptured obsidian and marine archaeology, a section dedicated to volcanology, and a reconstruction of the Bronze Age necropolis as well as amphoras, vases, and the famous theater masks.

▼ The Castle of Lipari built by the Spanish.

INDEX

SUPPLEMENTAL INFORMATION